What You Should Know About COMMUNISM and Why

By the EDITORS OF SCHOLASTIC MAGAZINES

Adapted from the series of sixteen articles published under the same title in *Senior Scholastic* and *World Week*, November 1961–April 1962.

(Revised March 1964)

SCHOLASTIC BOOK SERVICES

Published by Scholastic Book Services, a division of Scholastic Magazines, Inc., New York, N. Y.

ACKNOWLEDGMENTS

The Editors gratefully acknowledge the assistance of the following individuals who served as consultants to Scholastic Magazines for the series of articles on which this book is based:

SAMUEL M. BROWNELL, Superintendent of Public Schools, *Detroit, Michigan*

WILLIAM HENRY CHAMBERLIN, writer, *Cambridge, Massachusetts*

RT. REV. MSGR. O'NEILL C. D'AMOUR, Associate Secretary, *National Catholic Education Association, Washington, D.C.*

EUGENE LYONS, Senior Editor, *The Reader's Digest, Pleasantville, N.Y.*

J. W. MAUCKER, President, *State College of Iowa, Cedar Falls, Iowa*

PHILIP E. MOSELY, *Council on Foreign Relations, Inc., New York City*

HENRY L. ROBERTS, Professor of History, *Russian Institute, Columbia University, New York City*

HOWLAND H. SARGEANT, President, *American Committee for Liberation, New York City*

JOHN W. STUDEBAKER, Vice President and Chairman of the Editorial Boards, *Scholastic Magazines, New York City*   Maps by Bruno Junker

Editor: Robert F. Wilson   Cover: Sovfoto

Single copy price 65¢. Quantity prices available on request.

Also available: *What You Should Know About Communism—And Why*, Edition I; illustrated; 128 pages; 50¢ per copy, less school discount for quantity purchases. Adapted from the series of articles published in *Junior Scholastic*. For information, write to Scholastic Book Services, 50 West 44th Street, New York 36, N. Y.

Contents

Introduction 5

1. The Communist System 13
2. Karl Marx and the Start of Communism 22
3. From Lenin to Stalin 36
4. Purges at Home, Expansion Abroad 46
5. The Cold War Under Stalin 56
6. Coexistence With Khrushchev 69
7. The Many Shades of Communism 84
8. Life Under Communism in the Soviet Union 92
9. Education, Cultural Life, and Religion
   in the U.S.S.R. 104
10. The Communist Victory in China 123
11. The Communist Pattern of Conquest 137
12. Why Do Some People Become Communists? 152
13. The Might of Communism 161
14. The Free World's Response 173
   A Chronology of Communism 187
   Pronunciation Guide 188
   Index 189

(Study Aids follow each chapter)

MAPS AND CHARTS

Communism on the March 8-9
How the Communist Party Controls
   the Soviet Government 15
Communism Expands in Europe 59
Divided Germany 61
Comparative Purchasing Power, in
   Time Worked (U.S.A. and U.S.S.R.) 93
Communism Expands in Asia 133

East Berlin teen-agers join in a heroic but futile bid for freedom during the June, 1953, revolt against Communist rule.

Introduction

Why Study Communism?

Communism is more than a theory. It is a fighting force that deeply affects the life of every one of us.

Americans pay billions of dollars in taxes every year, 60 per cent of which go to support immense armaments. Expansion of American Armed Forces has led to the first peacetime draft in the history of the nation, calling hundreds of thousands of young Americans into the Armed Services. These measures are needed to protect the country and the Free World from the threat of communism, and they will continue in force as long as the Cold War — the conflict between the Free World and the Communist World — lasts.

You owe it to yourself to learn all you can about communism. If you do — and a careful reading of this book will give you a good start — you will be helping to safeguard your freedom, the freedom of your country and of the other free countries of the world.

This book will not limit its analysis of communism to the Union of Soviet Socialist Republics, although as the first Communist power, as the dominant Communist power in today's world, and as the one about which most is known, the Soviet Union will be emphasized.

Two Giants of Communism

Since November 7, 1917, when a group of Communist revolutionaries violently seized power in tsarist Russia, the Union of Soviet Socialist Republics has been the center of world Communist power. Using economic and political techniques radically different from those of the Western democracies, the Soviet Union has, in almost 50 years since the Bolshevik Revolution, forged a strong economic system. Today that system provides the base upon which Soviet leaders draw in attempting to spread communism throughout the world. In the last 10 years, Soviet military might has been built to a position second only to that of the United States — a very close second indeed, according to some authorities.

China — the China of Mao Tse-tung — is another giant Communist power. With Soviet help, Mao's Chinese Communists seized power through civil war in 1949. Today more than 700,000,000 Chinese live under their rule.

Each of these two giants of communism, the Soviet Union and Communist China, possesses its own "satellites" — countries whose foreign and domestic policies they largely control. The U.S.S.R.'s grip on Hungary, Romania, Czechoslovakia, Bulgaria, East Germany, and Poland is firm. Yugoslavia and Albania, though Communist, have shown greater independence from Soviet authority.

Red China has also seized control of neighboring states, among them Tibet, North Vietnam, and North Korea. Albania, in southern Europe, also is more closely tied to Red China than to the Soviet Union. Cuba, 90 miles off the Florida coast of the United States, has gone Communist under the dictatorship of Fidel Castro. It looks to both the Soviet Union and Red China for economic help, and is getting it.

The Threat to the Free World

Free people everywhere must be alert to the dangers of communism and be prepared to combat them intelligently, without fear. If in our decisions we are motivated by fear, we could make dangerous piecemeal surrenders, or act rashly and perhaps end up using communism's own tactics.

What has the Soviet Union been doing that arouses the concern of the United States and many non-Communist nations? Already nearly a third of the human race has been brought, *against its will,* under the Communist yoke. By word and action, Soviet leaders have made clear their determination to destroy our form of society and to put Communist governments everywhere. Would they start a war to do this? Soviet Premier Nikita Khrushchev boasts of the destructive power at his command. He has told leaders of non-Communist nations how cities like Rome, Athens, and London could be reduced to ashes by his atomic missiles. But the U.S. government has made our position clear: we will retaliate. Thus our military might has so far deterred Khrushchev from seizing West Berlin and the Communist Chinese from invading Taiwan.

Khrushchev and his aides are thoroughly committed to the Communist doctrine. They are spending huge sums of money in an effort to spread their system throughout the world. Along with propaganda, they rattle their rockets and flex their atomic muscles to frighten nations into doing their bidding. These military threats are supplemented by other threats. During his visit to the United States in 1961, Khrushchev was asked by reporters what he meant when he said, "We will bury you." He replied he did not mean burial by bombs, but burial by political and economic victory. He said that the Soviet Union, by 1980, will outproduce us in all kinds of goods, and will thus become a shining example

Atlantic Ocean

GREAT
BRITAIN

NORWAY

SWEDEN

FINLAND

DENMARK

Lake Ladoga

WEST

EAST Berlin

GERMANY

ESTONIA

LATVIA

LITHUANIA

AUSTRIA CZECHOSLOVAKIA

POLAND

Moscow

SOVIET

HUNGARY

YUGOSLAVIA

ROMANIA

ALBANIA

BULGARIA

GREECE

Black Sea

TURKEY

Caspian Sea

Aral Sea

Tehran

IRAN

AFGHANISTAN

KASHMIR

PAKISTAN

NEPAL

New Delhi

**COMMUNISM
ON THE MARCH**

INDIA

Under Communist rule in 1938
Taken over by Communists after 1938
Not on map: CUBA, taken over
by Communists in January, 1959.

0   250   500   1000 Statute Miles

of the success of communism. The propaganda effect will be tremendous, he thinks, and nation after nation will be converted to communism.

In the meantime Khrushchev is not just sitting back and waiting for the example of Soviet "progress" to take effect. Like Lenin and Stalin before him, he is working hard to promote communism in other nations. Everywhere — especially in the underdeveloped nations of Asia, Africa, and South America — Soviet agents and local Communists are working to unseat existing governments. Soviet policy has long been to support independence movements in many areas of the world, to capitalize on the anticolonial feelings of the people. The Soviet leaders thus hope to win the emerging nations to their side in the Cold War and eventually to establish communism in them.

Seven Tests of Freedom

The menace of communism to our freedom is not new. Since 1917, when the Communists overthrew the first Russian democratic government (then only eight months old) and set up a Communist dictatorship, strong voices from the democracies have warned the world of the danger. One of the most eloquent voices raised in opposition to communism has been that of Winston Churchill, Prime Minister of Great Britain during World War II. He has set down these seven tests of man's freedom under government:

1. Is there the right to free expression of opinion, to opposition and criticism of the existing government?

2. Have the people the right to vote out a government of which they disapprove, and are constitutional means provided by which they can make their will known?

3. Are there independent courts of justice free from executive control, and free from threats of mob violence and association with any particular political party?

4. Will these courts administer well-established laws which are associated in the human mind with the broad principles of decency and justice?

5. Will there be equal justice for poor as well as for rich, for individuals as well as for government officials?

6. Will the rights of the individual be exalted?

7. Is the ordinary citizen free from the fear that a secret police organization under the control of a single political party will pack him off without fair or open trial?

In other words, the chief tests of freedom are whether citizens are permitted to think, speak, act, and work freely.

In the chapters that follow you will see how communism denies those freedoms and rights we take for granted, and which we must ever be on the alert to defend and protect.

Democracy's Challenge

This is a book about communism — not about democracy. When living conditions in a Communist country are described, the reader should not assume that there are no shortcomings in the standard of living in many non-Communist countries. For example, the description of housing shortages in the Soviet Union should not be taken to mean that housing is adequate in every democratic country. On the other hand when it comes to the important "living condition" of freedom for the individual, there can be no dispute that the citizens of a democracy have rights denied the person living under communism. That story, *What You Should Know about Democracy — and Why,* is told in a companion book (published by Scholastic Book Services, April 1964).

Why study communism? A look at the front page of your daily newspaper will give you the answer: because communism affects your daily lives — your present and your future; because upon a firm understanding of communism, its nature and its history, depends the fate of all mankind.

INTRODUCTION — STUDY AIDS

Words and Names to Understand

Cold War
Union of Soviet Socialist Republics
tsarist   Taiwan

satellites
propaganda
underdeveloped nations

Checkup Questions

1. Why is communism called a "fighting force"? How are Americans affected by this force?
2. What country was first taken over by the Communists?
3. Who set down seven tests of man's freedom under government?
4. What means are the Communists using in an attempt to spread their system throughout the world?
5. What deterrents have kept Khrushchev from seizing West Berlin and other areas of the world he would like to control?

Questions to Think About

1. What did Khrushchev mean when he said of the United States, "We will bury you"?
2. Why do Soviet leaders support independence movements in many areas of the world?
3. To what extent does the Soviet Union meet the seven tests of freedom? To what extent does the United States meet them?
4. Why is it important to learn all we can about communism?

Books and Pamphlets to Read

Paperback Books:

Brumberg, Abraham, ed.. *Russia under Khrushchev*. Praeger, 1962.
The Communist Blueprint for the Future. Dutton, 1962.
Cronyn, George, *A Primer on Communism*. Dutton, 1961.
Decter, Moshe, ed., *The Profile of Communism*. Collier, 1961.
Khrushchev's "Mein Kampf." Belmont, 1961.
Orwell, George, *Animal Farm*. New American Library, 1956.
Rostow, W. W., *The Dynamics of Soviet Society*. Mentor, 1954.
Schwartz, Harry, ed., *The Many Faces of Communism*. Berkley, 1962.

Other Books:

Douglas, William O., *Russian Journey*. Doubleday, 1956.
Fitzsimmons, Thomas, *et al., USSR*. HRAF, 1960.
Gunther, John, *Inside Russia Today*. Harper, 1958.
Rama Rau, Santha, *My Russian Journey*. Harper, 1959.

The Communist System

The governments of the world today fall into three broad groups: democratic, authoritarian, totalitarian. Within each group there are variations in the degree of power exercised by the government over the people.

The word "democracy" comes from the Greek words *demos,* meaning "people," and *krator,* meaning "ruler." A *democratic* government is a government by consent of the people. The people have the right to vote — to replace their leaders at elections. They have freedom to criticize the government openly and to disagree with its policies without fear of punishment.

An *authoritarian* government is one that is dominated by a single leader or a dictatorial group (the *authority*). It usually permits private ownership of property, but restricts freedom of political action, including freedom of expression.

A *totalitarian* government is one which exercises *total* control. This includes control of property, education, and the means of communication — newspapers, books, magazines, radio, TV, theater, motion pictures, and other forms of art. Even the job each person holds is controlled by the government.

The line between authoritarianism and totalitarianism is sometimes thin. Both are dictatorships of one person or a ruling group that cannot be changed by the orderly process of voting by the people. Neither system gives the people the opportunity for a peaceful change of government, or permits individuals to campaign or agitate for a change.

A Totalitarian System

The Communist system is the most totalitarian system in existence today. It exercises complete control over the lives of the people. When the Communists seized power in the Bolshevik Revolution of 1917, they immediately set about tightening their grip on all phases of life in the newly proclaimed Soviet Republic.

The basis of Communist organization was and is the proposition that the Communist Party, which controls the state, knows what is "best" for the people and acts as the "vanguard" of the people. Communists use state power to control not only an individual's political life, but his economic and social life as well.

Communism is all-embracing — it is a dogmatic belief, a political party, a form of government, an economic system, a system of control over the individual, and a world-wide conspiracy.

1. *Communism is a dogmatic belief.* According to the Communists, their system is destined to take control of the entire world. The dedicated Communist is certain that his system is the "wave of the future." To bring the day of communism's triumph nearer, he will use any means — treachery, falsification, or violence — to advance his cause. As a disciplined agent of the Communist movement, he is expected

14

POLITICAL STRUCTURE OF THE SOVIET UNION

THE COMMUNIST PARTY → CONTROLS → THE GOVERNMENT

FIRST SECRETARY (leader of the Communist Party)	Both Posts Held Today by Nikita S. Khrushchev	**CHAIRMAN** Council of Ministers (Premier)

Communist Party	Government
PRESIDIUM of the COMMUNIST PARTY (Top Ruling Group in the U.S.S.R.)	PRESIDIUM of the COUNCIL OF MINISTERS (inner cabinet)
COMMUNIST PARTY CENTRAL COMMITTEE	COUNCIL of MINISTERS (cabinet or executive branch of government)
CONGRESS of the COMMUNIST PARTY, U.S.S.R.	SUPREME SOVIET of the U.S.S.R.
COMMUNIST PARTY CONGRESSES (at republic level)	SOVIETS of the REPUBLICS
REGIONAL (Oblast) CONGRESSES	REGIONAL (Oblast) SOVIETS
DISTRICT (Rayon) CONGRESSES	DISTRICT (Rayon) SOVIETS
LOCAL PARTY ORGANIZATIONS	RURAL SOVIETS

Notes: 1. Lower Party organizations send delegates to next higher levels.
2. Soviets ("councils" or legislative bodies) are elected directly by the people, but candidates must be approved by the Party.

 Shows direction of control.

to follow the Party's orders rigidly and carry them out unquestioningly. The Party line, or policy, may change from time to time as to *method,* but the *goal* of communism — world domination — remains unchanged.

2. *Communism is a political party.* Communism controls all political life in Communist countries. Party membership is closely regulated to ensure 100 per cent obedience to the commands of the top Party leaders. In the Soviet Union, with a population of about 225,000,000, there are some 10,000,000 Communist Party members. A candidate for membership in the Party is accepted only after Party leaders have investigated his background and are satisfied that he is loyal to the regime. A Party member is expected to see that Party orders are carried out in all his daily contacts — at work, at home, in the schools, anywhere. It is his duty to report any breach of Party discipline by his fellow workers, friends, or members of his family.

In the Soviet Union, Communist Party organization is parallel to that of the government on both national and local levels. At the top is the First Secretary of the Party. He is in charge of the Party *Presidium,* a group consisting of 11 members who decide on important Party policies. The Presidium in turn directs the *Central Committee,* which has a membership of approximately 175 and which, theoretically, handles Party affairs between the biennial meetings of the Party Congress. The First Secretary is also in charge of the *Secretariat,* which controls the choice of Party secretaries (or leaders) all the way down to the local Party group, called the "cell."

3. *Communism is a form of government.* On the surface, a government in a Communist state is like any other government. It carries out administrative, judicial, and legislative functions. Communist government is basically different from democratic government, however, in that it serves merely as a "rubber stamp" for decisions that have already been made

by Party leaders. This applies to all laws, appointments, and actions of the various agencies of the Communist government. Persons of importance in the government are members of the Communist Party and subject to its discipline.

At present the highest official in the government of the U.S.S.R., Premier Khrushchev, is also the First Secretary of the Communist Party. He is Chairman of the Council of Ministers, which in turn directs the various ministries (or governmental departments), such as foreign affairs, economy, foreign trade, transportation, health, and others.

Nominally, the highest lawmaking body is the *Supreme Soviet of the U.S.S.R.*, which has almost 1,500 members, called "deputies," and two chambers: the Council (or Soviet) of the Union, and the Council of Nationalities. Membership in the Council of the Union is based on population. Deputies in the Council of Nationalities are selected on a geographical basis from the various republics that make up the U.S.S.R., and from smaller areas. The Supreme Soviet elects the Premier and the Supreme Court. However, since all the actions of the Supreme Soviet require the prior approval of the Party, the Supreme Soviet has become a rubber stamp for Party policy, controlled by the First Secretary.

Elections in Communist countries offer the voters only one "choice." For example, candidates for the Supreme Soviet and the local soviets, or legislative bodies, are nominated at meetings of trade unions, schools, and collective farms, under Party supervision. Party officials direct the choice of one nominee for each office, so his election is assured.

The Soviet magazine *U.S.S.R.* (March, 1962) expresses the official point of view on elections this way:

> Since the interests of the people and the Communist Party are one and the same, and since there are no antagonistic groups or classes, there is no reason for several candidates to appear on the ballot.

That's what it said!

4. *Communism is an economic system.* In the Soviet Union, the state has complete control of the economy. For all industries and for agriculture, the government sets production quotas.

Despite some relaxation of controls since Stalin's death, the Soviet wage earner is still largely a pawn of the state. It is the government that determines the number of people to be trained for specific jobs or professions, assigns work, sets wages, and approves promotions. A worker may quit if he gives two weeks' notice. He pays a stiff price, however, for quitting. He loses many social security benefits, and his accident and health insurance is restored only after he has worked at his new job for six months.

There are, to be sure, trade unions in the U.S.S.R. But the function of the Soviet trade unions — unlike those in free countries — is mainly to enforce production quotas, and to serve as a disciplinary arm of the Party and government. The

Premier Khrushchev addresses the 22nd Congress of the Soviet Communist Party in October, 1961. At this meeting Khrushchev announced that by 1980 the Soviet Union would overtake the United States both in production and in the standard of living.

management metes out penalties for tardiness and absenteeism. No strikes are permitted. Quotas and prices of most consumer goods are fixed by the government.

Economic policies vary somewhat from one Communist nation to another. In Yugoslavia, for example, farmers are no longer forced to give up their land and join government-run collective farms. The same is true in Poland, a Soviet satellite, where most of the peasants own the land they work. In Poland there are also independent craftsmen, such as shoemakers, tailors, and barbers. However, industry is 90 per cent owned and operated by the state.

5. *Communism is a system of control over the individual.* In addition to controlling the people's political and economic life, a Communist government makes special efforts to mold people's thinking. The Secretariat of the Soviet Communist Party has a special section called AGITPROP (Agitation and Propaganda) which has been set up to indoctrinate the

people. Through the use of all channels of communication — newspapers, magazines, books, radio, TV, motion pictures, posters, literature, art, music, the theatre, the schools, Communist Party local groups — this agency carries on propaganda to support current government drives. These drives may take various forms, such as anti-U.S. campaigns, crusades against religion, or pressure for increased production.

6. *Communism is a world-wide conspiracy.* Soviet Russia extends its influence through a network of 90 Communist parties throughout the world, including the United States. In countries where the Communist Party has been declared illegal, it operates underground. Until recently, all of these parties received instructions from Moscow as to their programs of action. They sent delegates to international Communist Party meetings or congresses, held every two years. At the October, 1961 Party Congress in Moscow, there were delegates from Communist parties in 83 countries. Today some Communist parties (in North Vietnam, North Korea, and Albania) owe their allegiance to the Communist leaders of China.

The work of the Communist parties in foreign countries is supplemented by the activities of Moscow or Peiping agents, whose tasks may include recruiting local supporters, getting control of political organizations, provoking disturbances and riots, or working quietly to influence elections. When the political climate is favorable, these agents may incite an armed uprising, leading to the overthrow of a local government and its replacement by a Red regime.

Such, then, is the nature of communism — a system that suppresses and intimidates the individual, instills in people a fear of saying or doing anything that might displease Party leaders, keeps its leaders in power by means of dictatorship, and is committed to spreading itself throughout the world.

CHAPTER 1 — STUDY AIDS

Words and Names to Understand

authoritarian	Central Committee	Supreme Soviet
totalitarian	Secretariat	Party line
Presidium	Council of Ministers	collective farms

Checkup Questions

1. What are the three broad groups of governments in today's world? What is the role of the individual in each?
2. Why is communism said to be "all-embracing"?
3. What is the goal of communism?
4. What are the obligations of a Communist Party member?
5. Describe some of the restrictions on workers in the U.S.S.R.
6. What is the function of AGITPROP?
7. What are the duties of Soviet agents in foreign countries?
8. Why is Party membership so closely regulated?

Questions to Think About

1. How do elections in the U.S.S.R. differ from those in the U.S.?
2. To what extent do the people of the Soviet Union have a voice in the government?
3. How do U.S. trade unions differ from those in the Soviet Union?
4. By what means do the Communists attempt to control men's minds?

Books and Pamphlets to Read

Paperback Books:

Cronyn, George, *A Primer on Communism*. Dutton, 1961; Ch. 2.
Decter, Moshe, ed., *The Profile of Communism*. Collier, 1961; pp. 45-48.
Djilas, Milovan, *The New Class*. Praeger, 1957; pp. 37-102.
Khrushchev's "Mein Kampf." Belmont, 1961; pp. 135-146 and 182-208.
Lovenstein, Meno, *Capitalism, Communism, Socialism*. Curriculum Resources, 1962; Ch. 4.
Schwartz, Harry, ed., *The Many Faces of Communism*. Berkley, 1962; Ch. 1.

Other Books:

Ebenstein, William, *Today's Isms*. Prentice-Hall, 1961.
Fainsod, Merle, *How Russia Is Ruled*. Harvard University Press, 1953.
Fitzsimmons, Thomas, *et al.*, *USSR*. HRAF, 1960; Chs. 11 and 12.
Rostow, W. W., *The Dynamics of Soviet Society*. Mentor, 1954; pp. 60-89.

2

Karl Marx and the Start of Communism

The intellectual spark that ignited the Communist Revolution in Russia, in 1917, was furnished by Karl Marx (1818-1883). Marx was born in Trier, in the German Rhineland, and studied at German universities. He was an avid reader of philosophy and economics, and the more he observed the world around him, the more discontented he became.

At the age of 24 Marx went to Paris, where he met Friedrich Engels, son of a wealthy factory owner. The younger Engels and he were active in groups that believed in *socialism* — the idea that factories and other means of production should be owned by the government in the name of all the people.

In Paris, Marx heard of a new and fateful word, "communism," derived from the Latin word *communis*, meaning "belonging to all." Marx used the new word in the title and opening sentence of his first important writing, *The Communist Manifesto*, which he and Engels published in 1848.

The *Manifesto* begins on this note: "A specter is haunting Europe today — the specter of communism."

The *Manifesto* called on workingmen everywhere to rise up in revolt against the owners and managers of factories, mines, stores, and the means of public transportation. "Workers of the world, unite!" the *Manifesto* cried. "You have nothing to lose but your chains."

In the *Manifesto* and in his other writings, Marx represented the history of mankind as a series of changes from one form of "exploitation" to another. He declared that it was the custom for a *ruling* minority in a country to "exploit," or take economic and political advantage of, a ruled majority. His thinking along these lines was influenced by the ideas of the German philosopher, Georg Hegel (1770-1831).

History according to Marx

As Marx described history, man had originally lived in a state of "primitive communism." The land belonged to everyone, and each man kept the fruits of his labors. Then some stronger individuals got control of the land and forced the weaker ones to work for them. This led to slavery, under which powerful men owned both the land and the people who worked it. The slavery of the ancient Roman society gave way to the feudalism of the Middle Ages, with local rulers controlling the lives of the peasants who worked for them and maintaining private armies to protect their property rights. Feudalism, in turn, was replaced by capitalism.

Under capitalism Marx saw an inevitable struggle between those who owned capital — land, factories, machinery — and those who worked with their hands. Marx maintained that the workers do not receive the full return for their work because the capitalists keep the profit. Accordingly, a "class struggle" would develop between the "bourgeoisie" (the capitalists) and the "proletariat" (the wage earners). He predicted that this struggle would in time lead to a revolu-

Karl Marx, whose theories form the basis of communism, believed that *all* human development is shaped by material forces. According to Marxist doctrine, there is no God; neither is there a soul.

tion in which the proletariat would triumph and overthrow the capitalist system.

Marx described the way this revolution was to be brought about in his most famous work, *Das Kapital.* He declared that the rich would become richer and fewer, and that the poor would become poorer and more numerous. He contended that capitalism carried the seeds of its own destruction; that by the very nature of industrial progress the workers would be brought closer together, until finally they would revolt and substitute public for private ownership.

Marx's influence in the European Socialist movement continued to grow after his death in London, in 1883. It was particularly felt in Europe, where many of the hard-pressed factory workers or mill hands believed that Marxism supplied all the answers. Marx's writings had a lesser effect in the United States, because class distinctions were less rigid in the New World and opportunities for the individual to improve his economic and social status were not so limited. (Millions of persons immigrated to America from Europe precisely for that reason.)

There were many fallacies in Marxism (Marx's theory), and these were proved by the course of events:

• Marx was certain that the workers' revolution would come only after capitalism had reached its highest stage of development. Actually, Communist revolutions have occurred only in countries where capitalism was in an early phase, as in Russia, or in countries where capitalism had not even started to develop, as in China.

• The heart of Marx's doctrine — that poverty would become more widespread as wealth was concentrated in the hands of fewer and fewer people — has been completely refuted by the course of events in the United States and most of Western Europe, where the living standard of the wage earner has steadily risen and extremes of high and low income have tended to level off. Important causes for this are: (1) efficient production under the capitalist system; (2) agreements between labor and management; (3) minimum wage and hour laws; and (4) the income tax.

• Marx failed to make sufficient allowance for the idealistic impulses that move men. He did not take into consideration the vital force generated by man's religious feelings or the power of nationalism — his love of country.

• Most historians agree that the capitalist system, as it existed in the 19th century, was not quite so bad as Marx painted it. Moreover, it was later to undergo great changes because of three factors that Marx failed to take sufficiently into account: (1) the advance of scientific invention and technology; (2) the enactment of welfare and social legislation; and (3) the increased power and influence of trade unions.

Even before World War I some Socialists in Western Europe, realizing that the facts of everyday life did not correspond with Marx's theories, placed their hopes in *evolution* toward public ownership of the means of production rather than in *revolution*, as Marx did.

The Russian Background

At first glance, Russia seemed — by Marx's own standards — to be a country poorly suited for a Communist revolution. The industrial working class was very much smaller in proportion to the population than it was in Great Britain, Germany, and some of the other countries of Western Europe. Although industry and mining were developing rapidly elsewhere at the end of the 19th century, the Industrial Revolution had only scratched the surface of Russia's vast natural resources.

But there were factors that made Russia more vulnerable to revolution than other European countries. To begin with, the huge Russian Empire included many non-Russian nationalities — Poles, Finns, Lithuanians, and others — speaking a variety of languages and feeling more or less hostile to the tsarist state. Next, the standard of living was much lower in Russia than in Western Europe. Wages were low, and working conditions were bad. The mass of the people had little to lose, and there was always the hope that their lot might be improved by a change in the system.

The peasant in Western Europe, like the American farmer, was apt to be conservative in his point of view. He had held his land for several generations, and he looked with disfavor on riotous mobs and demonstrations in the big towns. But not so in Russia. There the peasant class seethed with discontent. Even though Tsar Alexander II had abolished serfdom in 1861, about one fourth of the land — often the best land — was still concentrated in large private estates. Also, most of these landowners were sharply distinguished from the peasants by habits, education, and standard of living.

The Russian middle class was small and weak, and was prevented from taking an active part in politics because of the vast power of the central government under the tsarist autocracy. In addition, many members of the Russian educated class saw clearly the social injustice of the tsarist system. They felt that a sweeping change, such as a revolution, was the only hope.

The Rise of Lenin

The man who did more than any other to translate the theory of Marx into the reality of the Russian Revolution was Vladimir Ilyich Ulyanov (1870-1924), better known by his assumed name of Lenin. (Most Russian revolutionaries used false names to throw the police off their trail.)

Lenin was the son of a district school inspector in the Volga River town of Simbirsk (later renamed Ulyanovsk, in Lenin's honor). His older brother Alexander, a student at the University of St. Petersburg, was hanged for taking part in a plot against the life of Tsar Alexander III. Lenin studied law at the same university, but never practiced it; instead, he soon became a professional revolutionary, living off his meager earnings from writings and translations. While still a young man, Lenin was arrested by the *Okhrana* (the tsarist secret police) and sent to Siberia, where he lived for three years. Later he went to Germany to publish a newspaper, *Iskra (The Spark)*, which was illegally distributed in Russia. At various times he lived in France, Switzerland, and Britain, subsisting on the small sums his illegal Russian Social Democratic Party could spare for the support of its representatives abroad.

From the beginning, Lenin was a dogmatic Marxist. His interpretation of Marxism, however, was one that Marx himself might not have approved. Lenin laid great stress on one phrase of Marx: "the dictatorship of the proletariat." But he thought of it not in terms of dictatorship *by* the proletariat, or wage earners, but rather as the dictatorship (of a minority party) *over* the proletariat and all other classes. As Lenin saw it, once the capitalist system was overthrown, this dictatorship would be set up and would continue until the final stage of utopian communism was reached. At that point, said Lenin, all classes would be abolished and everyone would give according to his abilities and receive according to his needs. Lenin also emphasized the importance of building a secret, highly disciplined party of professional revolutionaries as the driving force of revolutionary action.

In these two ideas — the dictatorship of the proletariat, which excluded political and civil rights and liberties for other classes; and a highly organized, tightly disciplined political party — one can see the germ of the totalitarian government that has since developed in the Soviet Union.

Most Marxian Socialists charge that Soviet communism has betrayed true Marxism. They contend that while Marx placed great stress on the development of the individual, Lenin increased the repressive power of the state. Years before he was associated with Lenin in the Soviet government, Leon Trotsky (1879-1940), one of the most famous of the Russian Marxist revolutionaries, voiced a strikingly prophetic criticism of the application of Lenin's theories:

> The Party organization would . . . substitute itself for the Party as a whole; then the Central Committee would sub-

Hundreds were killed on "Bloody Sunday," in 1905, when soldiers fired on a peaceful march of petitioners to the Tsar.

CULVER

stitute itself for the organization; and finally a single dictator would substitute himself for the Central Committee.

Lenin's early concept of the developing revolution embraced many ideas that non-Socialist liberals would have supported, such as: a freely elected constituent assembly, universal suffrage, guarantees of personal and civil liberties, and social legislation. These items were included in the original program of the Russian Social Democratic Party, prepared by Lenin and an older Marxist, Georgi Plekhanov, for adoption at the First Party Congress, held in Brussels and London in July and August, 1903.

The Russian Social Democratic Party at that time was split into *Bolshevik* and *Menshevik* wings. These terms come from the Russian words for "majority" *(bolshinstvo)* and "minority" *(menshinstvo)* and derived from the fact that at one Party Congress Lenin won the support of the majority. There were other occasions when he was in a minority. Actually, because of the conditions under which the Party worked, it would be hard to say which group really had more followers.

The March of Revolution

In the winter of 1904-1905, a spirit of increasing unrest swept the Russian Empire. An unpopular war with Japan sparked discontent. When, on January 22, 1905, a large number of workers led by an Orthodox priest, Father Gapon, approached the St. Petersburg Winter Palace with a petition addressed to Tsar Nicholas II, Cossack troops opened fire and killed more than 500 of the unarmed petitioners. The aftermath of this "Bloody Sunday" was a rash of popular demonstrations, peasant riots, seizure of landlord property, mutinies in the army and navy, and, in October, a nationwide general strike. This induced the Tsar to grant a constitution providing for a national parliament, the *Duma*.

The establishment of the constitution had the effect of driving a wedge between the liberals on one side and the revolutionaries on the other. The revolutionary forces had become disorganized, and for a while the movement was checked. An armed uprising in December, led by the Bolsheviks in Moscow, failed. The revolutionaries dissolved the *soviet* (Russian word for "council") which they had set up in St. Petersburg as a center of their activities. Bit by bit, the government asserted itself in reestablishing order throughout the country. The tsarist regime, after being in a state of deadlock with the first two Dumas, felt strong enough to arrest some Socialist deputies. The election laws were revised in such a way that the third and fourth Dumas were quite manageable by the regime. The lawmaking body became the instrument of the aristocracy and property-owning classes.

But the respite for the tsarist government was short. The uprising in 1905 proved to be, as Lenin once said, just a dress rehearsal for the Revolution of 1917.

Russian tsarism may well have signed its own death warrant when, on August 1, 1914, the government ordered the mobilization that preceded World War I. At first many liberals and some Socialists approved the war because Russia was allied with democratic Britain and France, but popular enthusiasm waned as casualty lists lengthened and German armies drove into Russian territory.

The upper classes were aroused as news spread of court intrigues — particularly the influence of the self-styled "monk," Gregory Rasputin, on the highstrung Tsarina Alexandra. He gained her favor by using his so-called healing powers on Alexis, the heir apparent, who suffered from hemophilia. Rasputin's power over the government became so great that many in court circles were envious of him and thought him an evil designer. In December, 1916, three noblemen murdered him. There were whispers about a

Alexander Kerensky (right), head of the provisional government, reviews troops during the summer of 1917. Since 1940 he has lived in the U.S., helping Russian emigrants and writing books about communism and the 1917 revolutions.

coup d'état to save Russia from the weak Tsar and the strong-willed Tsarina, but nothing happened. It took what seemed to be a small disturbance to reveal how feeble the autocracy had actually grown.

The disturbance occurred early in March, 1917, when bread riots started in working-class districts of the capital, Petrograd (now Leningrad). The Tsar was outside the city at general staff headquarters, commanding the army; so Petrograd authorities decided to call out troops to suppress the demonstrations. After some hesitation, the troops refused to fire on the crowds. What had started as a local riot was now a revolution.

Of all the great revolutions in history, the fall of the 300-year-old Romanov dynasty was one of the most spontaneous, unorganized, and leaderless. The leading revolutionaries were in prison or in exile — Lenin in Switzerland, Leon Trotsky in the United States. The Duma tried to assume leadership, but with little success. Real power soon passed into the hands of the Petrograd Soviet of Workers and Soldiers Deputies, which had been brought to life again to coordinate the strike movement as in 1905. Similar soviets sprang up in Moscow and other major cities, and eventually took shape elsewhere in the country and in the army. These soviets were not at first under Bolshevik control. The majority of their deputies belonged to the more moderate revolutionary parties — the Social Revolutionaries and the Mensheviks.

The provisional (temporary) government set up after the abdication of the Tsar was at first composed mainly of liberals, with a moderate Social Revolutionary lawyer, Alexander Kerensky, as minister of justice. As the tide of revolution rose, the liberals were unable to lead it, and Kerensky

In July, 1917, the Bolsheviks made a premature bid for power. Lenin-inspired riots in Petrograd killed 400 people.

carried on with an administration made up partly of Social Revolutionaries and Mensheviks.

In a dramatic move, Lenin returned to Russia to lead the Bolshevik forces. His trip, by armored railway car from Switzerland across Germany, was arranged by the German government. The Germans were then at war with Russia, and they knew that Lenin would act to end the war.

Lenin arrived in St. Petersburg on April 16, 1917, and announced a program of "no confidence" in the provisional government, opposition to the "imperialist" war, and all-out social revolution. Actually, Lenin took advantage of the freedoms permitted under the Kerensky government in order to destroy the government.

The fall of the Tsar left a vacuum that the well-meaning but weak provisional government could not fill. Widespread social revolt took more extreme forms as the temper of the revolution mounted:

• The armed forces refused to fight and began to disintegrate as the peasant soldiers returned to their villages.

• The industrial workers became more unruly and extreme in their demands on the factory owners.

• The peasants began to divide up the lands of the big estates.

• The non-Russian peoples in the population (Poles, Ukrainians, Latvians, Lithuanians, Estonians, Finns, Georgians) demanded self-rule.

Above all, Russia was defeated and exhausted by World War I (1914-1917). In the resulting chaos and demoralization, the Bolsheviks took over.

The Bolsheviks in Command

The attempt of General Kornilov, commander in chief of the armed forces, to bring off a conservative *coup d'état* to gain control, failed in September and speeded up the swing

Bolshevik troops storm the Winter Palace in Petrograd. Except for one shell fired from the cruiser *Aurora*, the fall of Kerensky's government was accomplished with small arms.

toward the Bolsheviks. On November 6-7 the Communist Revolution, urged by Lenin since July and carefully planned by the Bolshevik Party, took over Petrograd with little bloodshed. Kerensky fled to the war front to rally troops to his support, but failed and left Russia. (He has been living in the United States since 1940.)

The new regime, with Lenin as Chairman of the Council of Commissars and Trotsky as Commissar for Foreign Affairs, appealed to all participants in World War I for immediate peace negotiations and opened direct discussions with Germany for an armistice. Within Russia, the Bolshevik regime nationalized natural resources and land, much of which was to be turned over to the peasants for cultivation without hired labor; it proclaimed control of industry by the workers, and government seizure of the banks. For the first time in history a government made up of Marxist revolutionaries was in control of a huge country.

CHAPTER 2 — STUDY AIDS

Words and Names to Understand

socialism	bourgeoisie	Bolshevik
"primitive communism"	proletariat	Menshevik
feudalism	Marxism	Duma
capitalism	autocracy	Romanov dynasty

Checkup Questions

1. How did Karl Marx describe the history of mankind?
2. Why were Marx's writings less influential in the United States than in Europe?
3. What factors made Russia vulnerable to a revolution?
4. What is meant by the phrase, "dictatorship of the proletariat"?
5. What did Lenin envision as the final stage of communism?
6. What took place on "Bloody Sunday"? What were the repercussions?
7. What actions did Lenin take after he assumed power in November, 1917?

Questions to Think About

1. On what basis did Marx conclude that capitalism would give way to communism? What factors did he fail to take into account?
2. What did Trotsky feel would be the probable effect of Lenin's theories? Was he correct?
3. What was the first program of the Russian Social Democratic Party? Why did this party split into two factions, the Bolsheviks and the Mensheviks?
4. What is the "heart" of Marx's doctrine? What has been the course of events in the United States that has refuted Marx's idea?

Books and Pamphlets to Read

Paperback Books and Pamphlets:

Decter, Moshe, ed., *The Profile of Communism.* Collier, 1961; pp. 19-30.

Lawrence, John, *A History of Russia.* Evergreen, 1960; Ch. 19.

Mayo, Henry B., *An Introduction to Marxist Theory.* Oxford.

Mendel, Arthur, ed., *Essential Writings of Marxism.* Bantam.

Moorehead, Alan, *The Russian Revolution.* Bantam.

Pares, Bernard, *Russia.* Mentor, 1949; Chs. 4 and 5.

Rauch, George von, *A History of Soviet Russia.* Praeger, 1957.

Seton-Watson, Hugh, *From Lenin to Khrushchev.* Praeger, 1960; Ch. 2.

Whitney, Thomas P., ed., *The Communist Blueprint for the Future.* Dutton, 1962; pp. 3-44 and 66-73.

3

From Lenin to Stalin

When Lenin seized power he faced a demoralized army, and a nation torn by war and revolution, and divided by class loyalties. His first step in establishing the dictatorship of the proletariat was to issue a decree expropriating — that is, taking over — the landed estates. Then, with Leon Trotsky, head of the Red Army and War Commissar, he set about to end the war with Germany.

Lenin and Trotsky asked the Germans for a peace conference, which was held at Brest-Litovsk in Poland. On March 3, 1918, the long, frequently interrupted negotiations were concluded. To Germany the Soviet government ceded Poland, the Baltic states, and the Ukraine.

The Civil War

On the domestic scene, meanwhile, things were going badly. Lenin's program for nationalization of private enterprises met with great resistance. It never could have been enforced in a country with a high standard of living. Even in

A Soviet artist's conception of the fall of Tsaritsyn (later Stalingrad, now Volgograd) in the civil war. Directing operations is Stalin, then a senior commissar in the Red Army.

Russia it appealed only to the poorer groups of the population.

The result was civil war between the Red (Communist) Russians and the White (anti-Communist) Russians. Some foreign aid was sent to the Whites. Great Britain and the United States sent troops to North Russia; France, to South Russia; and the United States and Japan, to eastern Siberia. This military intervention was on a small scale and involved little direct fighting with the Soviet army. None of these powers — with the possible exception of Japan — had any territorial aspirations in Russia. The intervention probably would not have occurred at all had it not been for the fear that the Germans might seize large stocks of Allied munitions and supplies that were stored in the Russian ports of Archangel, Murmansk, and Vladivostok.

The Soviets held North Central Russia throughout the civil war. The main centers of resistance were in Siberia and South

Lenin speaks to Red Square crowds on May 1, 1919. May Day
was selected by the Second International (see page 144) in
1889 as an international Labor Day. In the Soviet Union, May
Day is an official holiday marked by parades and speeches.

Russia. In the south, the strongest of the White armies, under
General Anton Denikin, swept across the Ukraine in the
summer of 1919 to Orel, a town less than 200 miles from
Moscow. However, Denikin's lines were so thin and widely
extended that the southern front quickly collapsed against
Soviet military forces. One of Denikin's generals, Peter
Wrangel, held out in the Crimea until November, 1920, as
did the leader of the White cause in Siberia, Admiral Alexander Kolchak. Kolchak was finally captured and shot.

By the end of 1920, armed resistance to the Soviet rule
had been reduced to scattered peasant guerrilla operations.
But that same year the Soviets faced a new war: Poland invaded Russia and, on May 6, captured Kiev. The city was
soon retaken by the Soviet armies, which marched to the
very gates of Warsaw but were routed by a Polish counteroffensive and driven from the country. A treaty signed at
Riga on March 18, 1921, ended the war.

War Communism

During this period (1917-1921), Soviet Russia lived under a system of so-called war communism. The state took over production and distribution. The peasants were ordered to turn in surplus grain and other foodstuffs, in exchange for manufactured goods. But the drastic Communist economic experiments had caused engineers and factory managers to leave the cities, and production dropped. When the peasants discovered that few consumer goods were to be had, they cut down on farm production. The result was starvation for the cities. Food and other goods were rationed. Cold and hunger were universal. People fled to the villages in search of food. Though hostilities had ceased, Soviet troops were used as labor battalions in such tasks as felling trees, building roads, loading and unloading freight cars.

Money rolled off the government printing presses and became worthless. The state halted interest payments on bonds and stocks. All private land was seized, and working-class families were moved into the homes of the well-to-do.

Private apartments were subdivided on the basis of one family to a room. Rich country homes were sacked and burned, or converted to public use.

Changes under the NEP

In spite of these stringent controls, the Soviet economy did not revive after the civil war, and war communism was abandoned. Growing unrest exploded in a series of peasant uprisings and a revolt of sailors and workers at a former Communist stronghold, the Kronstadt Naval Base, near Petrograd, on March 1, 1921.

The Kronstadt uprising was in no sense an attempt to restore capitalism. The insurgents called for freely elected soviets, freedom of speech and press — but only for Socialists and other radical groups. The sailors demanded abolition of special privileges for Communists, and a reform of the harsh laws controlling the peasants. Soviet troops finally put down the revolt on March 18.

The uprising hastened Lenin's introduction of the New Economic Policy (NEP). The system of making the peasant meet exorbitant and often unexpected production demands was replaced by setting a definite amount of grain which the peasant would have to give to the government. No longer would he have to surrender all his produce. This gave the peasant more freedom in the use of the land and — what had been lacking during the years of war communism — an incentive to produce.

Even so, famine struck. Millions of persons perished in 1921 and 1922, although the death toll would have been much higher had it not been for the substantial amounts of food supplied by the American Relief Administration, headed by Herbert Hoover.

The concession to the peasants led to other concessions. Freedom of trade inside the country was restored, and a surprising number of "Nepmen" — private merchants and traders

Lenin and Trotsky watch a demonstration during the winter of 1920. Although they often differed regarding the application of communism, Lenin until his death spoke highly of Trotsky.

— sprang up. A new currency was issued. Home building and the setting up of small factories were permitted. When foreign capitalists were invited to invest in Soviet enterprises, some people wrongly assumed that Soviet Russia was returning to capitalism. But even in these years of comparative economic freedom, the dictatorship of the Communist Party remained intact. The state retained full control of the big industries, and of all exports and imports.

From the first, communism had been forced on the people. The Soviet population never had a chance to decide in a free election whether it wanted the Communist system. Only one free election was ever held in the Soviet Union, and that was for a Constituent Assembly, which met on January 18, 1918.

The Assembly was promptly dissolved by the Bolshevik armed forces when it showed an anti-Bolshevik majority. (Only about 25 per cent of the delegates were Bolsheviks; 62 per cent belonged to the Social Revolutionaries and to moderate Socialist parties, and about 13 per cent to parties with more conservative programs.)

Lenin's Successor

Lenin, who had been ailing for several years, began to show signs of physical exhaustion in 1922. After a series of paralytic strokes, he died on January 21, 1924.

Before his final breakdown, Lenin composed a political testament, in which he warned of danger to Party unity from a clash between two of his colleagues: Trotsky and Stalin. He characterized Stalin as a "rough and disloyal" man who, in the post of General Secretary of the Party, had concentrated great power in his hands. Lenin urged that Stalin be removed from that post.

Immediately after Lenin's death — indeed, after his disability — a triumvirate of Stalin, Zinoviev, and Kamenev took over the Party leadership. These three men proved powerful enough to challenge Leon Trotsky — the most influential figure in the Revolution, second only to Lenin — and to force his dismissal from the post of War Commissar.

In 1925 Stalin turned against Zinoviev and Kamenev on the pretext that their policy toward the peasants was "too harsh." To oust Zinoviev and Kamenev from office, Stalin formed an alliance with the "right" or moderate wing in the Communist Party, headed by Premier Aleksei Rykov, *Pravda* editor Nikolai Bukharin, and Mikhail Tomsky, head of the Soviet trade unions.

Trotsky joined his old opponents Zinoviev and Kamenev, in a so-called "left" opposition. This was crushed by Stalin with the aid of his new allies from the "right wing." In 1927, Trotsky was exiled to Alma Ata, near the Chinese border. In

1929 he was expelled from the Soviet Union, and thereafter led a life of exile in Turkey, France, Norway, and Mexico, where he was murdered in 1940 by a secret agent of Stalin.

In 1928 Stalin broke his alliance with Rykov, Bukharin, and Tomsky, and eliminated their influence in the Party. By 1929 he had consolidated his power, and until his death in 1953 he was the absolute ruler of the Soviet Union and of the world-wide Communist movement.

Industrialism and Collective Farming

Under Stalin's dictatorship, from 1928 to 1953, tremendous changes occurred in the practice and meaning of communism. Soviet economic policy was directed toward two goals: the replacement of individual by collective farming; and the development of the country's heavy industries under a series of Five-Year plans.

When Stalin assumed power in 1928, he found that the peasants were not bringing enough grain to market to permit large-scale exports. This, in turn, deprived the government of money for needed imports. Surplus grain in the past had come largely from the landed estates, now swept away by the Revolution.

The government struck ruthlessly. Stalin broke the peasants' resistance by forcing them to pool their small landholdings into big collective farms. Here they worked under strict control, with the state dictating what crops they would raise and the prices they would be paid.

The *kulaks* (well-to-do peasants) were outlawed, their land and property taken away. Millions of men, women, and children were herded into freight cars and sent to forced labor in lumber camps, factories, and mines. In southern and southeastern Russia millions of others died of starvation in 1932-1933 — a famine caused not by extreme drought, but by the government's decision to "teach the peasants a lesson" when they slacked off in raising crops.

During the same period new factories were erected, often with technical advice from U. S. and German engineers. This was a time of severe belt-tightening for the Soviet people. Forced collectivization of farms and stepped-up industrialization drastically lowered the already marginal standard of living.

"A Man Without Pity or Mercy"

The passing of power from Lenin to Stalin had marked a moral degeneration of communism. Lenin, ruthless in achieving his ends, had a selfless devotion to his ideals. Even in the critical civil war days he permitted free debate within the ranks of the Communist Party. Personal flattery was unwelcome to him; he thought only in terms of his program. He dominated the Communist Party not by terror, but by force of personality.

Stalin, on the other hand, thought mainly in terms of building up his absolute personal power. He had killed every one of his six associates in the Politburo. His policy of forcibly driving the peasants into collective farms took a toll of millions of lives in famine and desperate resistance. He sent millions of people to their deaths and into slave labor camps in Siberia. Under his orders more than a million people were deported to forced labor camps from eastern Poland and the Baltic states.

George F. Kennan, U.S. diplomat and eminent scholar in Soviet history, has this to say of Stalin:

> This was a man of incredible criminality, of a criminality effectively without limits; a man apparently foreign to the very experience of love, without pity or mercy; a man in whose entourage no one was ever safe; a man whose hand was set against all that could not be useful to him at the moment; a man who was most dangerous of all to those who were his closest collaborators in crime.

CHAPTER 3 — STUDY AIDS

Words and Names to Understand

Politburo
Brest-Litovsk Conference
Riga treaty
war communism

Kronstadt uprising
New Economic Policy (NEP)
Constituent Assembly
Five-Year plans
kulaks

Checkup Questions

1. Why did the U.S. and other countries intervene in the civil war between the Whites and Reds? How did this war end?
2. Describe "war communism." Why was it put into effect?
3. What concessions were made to peasants and merchants under Lenin's NEP?
4. What were the goals of Stalin's economic policy? How did he try to attain them?

Questions to Think About

1. Why would it be difficult to bring about Lenin's program of government seizure of private property in a country with a high standard of living?
2. What basis is there for describing Stalin's rise to power as "ruthless"?
3. It has been stated that communism was imposed on the people of Russia. How was this possible?
4. Why did policies under the NEP cause foreigners to feel that Russia might be returning to capitalism?

Books, Pamphlets, and Articles to Read

Paperback Books and Pamphlets:

Jessup, John K., and the editors of *Life, Communism, the Nature of Your Enemy.* Time, Inc., 1962; pp. 6-36.

Lawrence, John, *A History of Russia.* Evergreen, 1960; Chs. 20 and 21.

Rostow, W. W., *The Dynamics of Soviet Society.* Mentor, 1954; pp. 27-49.

Seton-Watson, Hugh, *From Lenin to Khrushchev.* Praeger, 1960; Ch. 4.

Shub, David, *Lenin.* Mentor, 1948.

Whitney, Thomas P., ed., *The Communist Blueprint for the Future.* Dutton, 1962; pp. 74-99.

Wolfe, Bertram, *Three Who Made a Revolution.* Beacon, 1955.

Articles:

"Lenin: The Evil Genius Who Launched the Global Red Threat," Richard Harrity and Ralph G. Martin. *Look,* May 22, 1962.

4

Purges
at Home,
Expansion
Abroad

Two important developments occurred in the Soviet Union in the 1930's: the ruthless purges with which Stalin decimated the ranks of the Communist Party, and the expansion of Soviet communism beyond the boundaries of the Soviet Union.

The first is one of the darkest and most mysterious pages in history.

The second was made possible by the signing of the Nazi-Soviet pact in 1939, and the subsequent outbreak of World War II.

Early Purges

From the time the Communist Party seized power in Russia, Lenin and other leaders had been concerned about maintaining its revolutionary idealism. So long as the Communists were a small, persecuted band harried by the Tsar's police, no one was likely to join the movement for selfish reasons.

Conditions changed in November, 1917, when the former hunted revolutionaries became the new rulers. Many were now attracted to the Communist camp because of the privileges that came with membership in the ruling class.

One of the devices Lenin used to keep the Party pure was the *chistka* (purge), during which all members were strictly examined as to their ideas, their social origin (workers were preferred as Party members), and their behavior. Those who were found unworthy by the investigators were dropped from the rolls. Causes for expulsion included political disloyalty, drunkenness, embezzlement, and the holding of any religious faith. A purge ordered by the Eighth Party Congress in 1919 resulted in the expulsion of 100,000 members. A few years later 170,000 more were dropped.

Stalin's Purges

Under Stalin the *chistka* took a more sinister turn. During the 1930's the terror of the secret police system — midnight arrest, gruelling cross-examination, torture, banishment to forced labor, execution without trial — descended with its full weight on the Communist Party itself. (Hitherto such methods had been mainly reserved for persons suspected of anti-Soviet attitudes and activities.) Not since the time of Ivan the Terrible (1530-1584) had so many high state functionaries been destroyed. The purges — finally exposed as fraudulent by Khrushchev in a speech twenty years later, at the 20th Congress of the Communist Party in 1956 — are an awesome memorial to Stalin's all-powerful personal rule.

The purges were touched off on December 1, 1934, when a young Communist named L. Nikolaev shot and mortally wounded Sergei Kirov, head of the Leningrad organization of the Party. It is possible that the act was committed by Nikolaev either because of some personal quarrel with his victim or because of his disillusionment with the Soviet system.

Then again, the murder may have been "arranged" by Stalin himself, as Khrushchev intimated in a speech before the 22nd Communist Party Congress in 1961. Whatever the facts, the assassination was used as an excuse for killing hundreds of alleged White Russians who languished in prison, and for unloosing a reign of terror against suspected sympathizers with the banished Trotsky and his allies.

In August, 1936, Zinoviev, Kamenev, and 14 other prominent Bolsheviks were put on trial for plotting the murder of Kirov and trying to kill Stalin. There was a notable lack of convincing evidence, and some apparently false evidence. For example, one of the defendants told of meeting Trotsky's son, Sedov, in the lounge of the Hotel Bristol in Copenhagen — but there was no Hotel Bristol in Copenhagen at the time of the alleged meeting. Nevertheless, all sixteen of the accused "confessed" their guilt and were executed.

The second big trial, in February, 1937, resulted in 13 more death sentences. Most of the victims were Communists who were charged with being supporters of Leon Trotsky. There were stories of secret meetings abroad. A leading Bolshevik, Pyatakov, "confessed" that he had met Trotsky in Norway and that Trotsky told him of making an agreement with the leaders of Nazi Germany, promising them parts of Soviet territory in return for their help in overthrowing Stalin.

The Red Army was purged, too. In 1937 Marshal Tukhachevsky and seven high-ranking generals were arrested, tried secretly by a military tribunal, and executed by a firing squad. Most of their judges soon followed them.

The last big show trial, staged in March, 1938, led to the execution of former Premier Aleksei Rykov and of leading Communist theoretician Nikolai Bukharin, among others.

The most bizarre feature of this trial was the statement of a former head of the Soviet political police, Henrich Yagoda, that he had poisoned the noted Russian author, Maxim Gorky, and several prominent Soviet officials.

Party members stand trial during Stalin's purges of the 1930's. Thousands were expelled, imprisoned, or executed.

Khrushchev Denounces the Purges

No word of doubt or criticism of these trials was permitted to be published in the Soviet Union. Communist sympathizers in the United States and other countries followed the "Party line" and hailed the gruesome spectacles as a triumph of justice. Voices of doubt were raised, however, because of discrepancies in the evidence. A commission of inquiry, headed by the American educator and philosopher John Dewey, made an exhaustive examination of the alleged evidence of Trotsky's participation in the anti-Soviet plots. The Dewey commission's verdict: "Not guilty."

The charges of Nazi intrigues with the victims of the trials could never be substantiated. When the Allies captured Berlin in 1945 they were unable to find any documents concerning these matters in the Nazi archives.

Any illusion about the genuineness of the trials and the methods by which "confessions" were extracted was dispelled when Khrushchev, in his summing-up speech at the 22nd Congress of the Communist Party, in October, 1961, made this admission:

> Here among the delegates there are comrades—I do not wish to mention their names so as not to cause them pain—who for many years were in prison. They were persuaded—by certain methods—that they were either German or British or some other spies; and some of them confessed.

The German invasion of Poland, in September, 1939, setting off World War II, and the Soviet attack on Finland in November of the same year, marked a new turn in Soviet foreign policy. It had already been foreshadowed by the so-called nonaggression pact between the Soviet Union and Nazi Germany, concluded on August 23 of the same year. This pact is better described as a treaty to divide Eastern Europe between the Nazi and the Communist dictatorships. It contained a secret agreement assigning Latvia and Estonia to the Soviet and Lithuania to the German "sphere of influence." It permitted the annexation of Bessarabia, a province of Romania, by the Soviet Union. Poland was to be divided along the line of the rivers Narew, Vistula, and San. Later this deal was modified, so that Lithuania fell to the Soviet sphere and Germany got an enlarged share of Poland.

Two weeks after Poland's military resistance was broken by the German invasion on September 1, 1939, the Soviet Union occupied the eastern provinces of Poland with almost no fighting. Hundreds of thousands of Poles were deported to forced labor in Siberia, and the territory was finally incorporated in the Soviet Union.

Toward the end of 1939, the Soviet government demanded a big slice of territory from Finland. The Finns refused, and the U.S.S.R. invaded their land. Though greatly outnumbered, the Finns defended themselves with great courage and skill. For this act of aggression, the League of Nations expelled the Soviet Union from its membership; but none of the Western nations offered to help Finland, and that country was forced to conclude an unsatisfactory peace with the Soviets in March, 1940. The Soviet Union annexed Finland's Isthmus of Karelia, with the important town of Vyborg, and established a naval base at Hangö. But Finland at least saved its independence. The three small Baltic nations — Latvia, Lithuania, and Estonia — were less fortunate. They were absorbed by the U.S.S.R. in June. At the same time Romania was forced by threat of Soviet military action to give up Bessarabia and northern Bukovina.

The uneasy alliance between the two totalitarian powers — Nazi Germany and the U.S.S.R. — persisted for nearly two years. The Soviet government congratulated Hitler on the capture of Paris and denounced England as "imperialist." Communist parties throughout the world parroted the Moscow line, although some individual Communists were so disillusioned by the pact with Hitler that they quit the Party.

A turning point in Soviet-Nazi relations was the visit by Foreign Commissar Molotov to Berlin in November, 1940, to discuss the possibility of Moscow's joining the Berlin-Rome-Tokyo Axis. Molotov demanded a stiff price: the departure of German troops from Finland; a treaty with Bulgaria; a Soviet military base on the Straits of the Bosporus; and Japan's surrender of her oil and mining rights in Northern Sakhalin. Molotov never received an answer to these proposals. The real answer came on June 22, 1941, when the German armies invaded the Soviet Union on a long front extending from Finland to the Black Sea.

World War II

Finland and Romania, previous victims of Soviet aggression, took part in the war on the side of Germany, as did Italy and Hungary. Britain and the United States concluded an alliance with the Soviet and sent them large quantities of military supplies, partly through the North Russian ports of Murmansk and Archangel, partly by way of Iran.

The German forces, paced by armored units, rapidly over-ran eastern Poland, the Baltic states, and much of the Ukraine and central Russia. They took thousands of prisoners at Kiev and south of Moscow. That winter the Soviet army, invigorated by fresh Siberian troops, stopped Hitler's forces outside of Moscow. But the Germans had occupied most of the Ukraine and held Leningrad in a strangling blockade.

The second big German advance, in the summer of 1942, reached Stalingrad (now Volgograd). After months of fierce fighting, the German troops there were encircled and forced to surrender. But Stalingrad was virtually destroyed.

Strategically the war may have been lost by the Germans' failure to capture Moscow in the first drive. Their over-extended lines made them an easy prey to the pincer move-ments of the Soviet counteroffensive. The Soviets regained most of the territory held by the Germans earlier in the year.

From then on the Germans were on the defensive. By the summer of 1944, the Soviet Army had advanced deep into Poland and stood on the Vistula, where it paused long enough to let the Germans destroy the underground nation-alist Polish forces that rose in revolt against the Germans in Warsaw. By the spring of 1945, with the Americans and British invading Germany from the west, the Soviet armies were on the shores of the Oder River. By April 29 they had fought their way to Berlin, where Adolf Hitler committed suicide amid the ruins of what he had thought would be his "thousand-year empire."

The Big Wartime Conferences

Up to 1962 there had been no general peace treaty ending World War II. This was because of the division of Germany into non-Communist and Communist zones, and the serious differences between the Soviet Union and the Western powers. The shape of the postwar world was determined largely by the course of the war and by Stalin's determination to set up Communist-ruled states wherever his armies advanced. During the war years the leaders of the Soviet Union, the United States, and Great Britain met three times. These conferences were held at Teheran, in Iran (December, 1943); Yalta, in the Soviet Union (February, 1945); and Potsdam, in Germany (July-August, 1945).

Of these meetings, perhaps the most important was Yalta. At that meeting, Roosevelt, Stalin, and Churchill agreed that

At Yalta, in 1945, British Prime Minister Churchill, U.S. President Roosevelt, and Stalin agreed on plans for a postwar world—which the Soviets ultimately violated (see page 150).

the Soviet Union should receive the same territory — at the expense of Poland — which it would have gained as a result of its deal with Hitler. Poland was to be compensated by German territory to the north and west of its former frontiers. The provisional government of Poland was to be "reorganized on a broader democratic basis" and was to be pledged to "the holding of free and unfettered elections as soon as possible." (The background of these conditions and their violations by the U.S.S.R. will be discussed in the next chapter.)

Under the Yalta agreement, the three powers also agreed to cooperate "in assisting the peoples of the former Axis satellite states of Europe to solve by democratic means their pressing political and economic problems." Temporary governments were to be formed, "broadly representative of all democratic elements in the population and pledged to the earliest possible establishment through free elections of governments responsive to the will of the people."

Another feature of the Yalta agreement, not announced at the time, was a Soviet promise to enter the war against Japan "two or three months after Germany has surrendered." In return, the U.S.S.R. was to receive South Sakhalin and the Kurile Islands, in addition to port and railway facilities in Manchuria and the lease of Port Arthur as a naval base.

As the war ground to its close, it became ever clearer that Stalin had no trust in any ally, and that he believed that the defeat of Germany and Japan would make the Soviet Union the strongest military power in the world. It was also apparent that he would not tolerate any democratic institutions in the countries his armies had overrun. His ambitions for additional conquests were far from satisfied.

Indeed, he had been fighting a separate war, for separate aims of his own. The full impact of Soviet ambitions, and of the changed balance of power in Europe and Asia, was only gradually to be realized as the hopes for peace and cooperation gave way to Stalin's Cold War.

CHAPTER 4 — STUDY AIDS

Words and Names to Understand

chistka	annexation	Yalta Conference
nonaggression pact	League of Nations	Postdam Conference
sphere of influence	Teheran Conference	balance of power
	Bosporus Northern Sakhalin	

Checkup Questions

1. What two important developments occurred in the Soviet Union in the 1930's?
2. What was the *chistka?* How was it used in the 1920's? 1930's?
3. How was Eastern Europe to be divided between the Soviet Union and Germany?
4. What was the result of the Russo-Finnish War?
5. What was the turning point in Soviet-Nazi relations in 1940?
6. Why did Finland and Romania join Germany in World War II?
7. Why has there been no peace treaty ending World War II?

Questions to Think About

1. Why did prominent Bolsheviks "confess" their guilt during the purge trials, despite a lack of evidence against them?
2. Why was the nonagression pact of 1939 a new departure in Soviet foreign policy?
3. How do the Communist purges illustrate the differences in legal procedure between Communist and free societies?

Books and Pamphlets to Read

Paperback Books:

Decter, Moshe, ed., *The Profile of Communism.* Collier, 1961; pp. 61-66.
Isenberg, Irwin, *The Soviet Satellites.* Scholastic Book Services, 1963.
Koestler, Arthur, *Darkness at Noon* (novel). Signet, 1941.
Lawrence, John, *A History of Russia.* Evergreen, 1960; Ch. 22.
Pares, Bernard, *Russia.* Mentor, 1949; Chs. 15, 16, and 17.
The Soviet Union. Scholastic Book Services, 1962. Ch. 5.
Seton-Watson, Hugh, *From Lenin to Khrushchev.* Praeger, 1960; Chs. 8 and 10.

Other Books:

Armstrong, John A., *The Politics of Totalitarianism: The Communist Party from 1934 to the Present.* Random House, 1961.
Byrnes, James, *Speaking Frankly.* Harper, 1947.
Harcave, Sidney, *Russia, a History.* Lippincott, 1956.

5

The
Cold War
Under Stalin

In the thick forestland near Smolensk, in western Russia, lies the village of Katyn. One bleak day during World War II, 8,000 officers of the Polish army were murdered there.

The identity of the murderers has never been officially established, although the weight of evidence is against the Soviet Union. The prisoners were in the hands of both German and Soviet armies at various times; and after the Nazis invaded Russia they announced, in the spring of 1943, that they had found the mass graves. When officials of the Polish government in London asked that the International Red Cross investigate the matter, Moscow broke off diplomatic relations with the government in exile. Later the Soviet government accused the Germans of responsibility for the Katyn massacre. This act of wholesale butchery was included in the list of war crimes at the Nuremberg trials, but it was never brought to prosecution — another indication that the true criminals in this particular atrocity might perhaps be sought in Moscow rather than in Berlin.

Following the break in relations with the legitimate Polish government, the Soviet government marched back into Poland, drove out the German forces, and installed a "provisional Polish government," with a hard core of Moscow-trained Communists. The promises at Yalta of "reorganization" of this puppet government and of "free and unfettered elections" were treated as scraps of paper. After ousting the Germans, the U.S.S.R. waited almost two years before holding a Polish national election in January, 1947. This election, which the Communist candidates "won," was the occasion for so much violence and fraud that it aroused protests from the Western powers, to no avail. Two hundred people were murdered, 1,000 more were arrested, and 5,000 families were evicted from their homes — all for failing to acknowledge the "legality" of the Communist victory.

Guerrilla warfare against the Communist government in Poland persisted for several years, as it did in Lithuania and elsewhere. But, as the rebels received no support from abroad, resistance was eventually stamped out and Poland fell under the rule of a foreign-directed totalitarian terror. There was a special tragedy in the fate of Poland. It had been the first country to take up arms against the Nazis and the first victim of the Nazi-Soviet pact of August 23, 1939. Poland's subjection to the Communist take-over was the first of a series of events that led to the Cold War.

The Cold War has not been entirely bloodless. One needs only to recall the casualty lists in Korea, where U.S. and other U.N. soldiers died (see page 65). But the Cold War has been fought to a considerable extent with political, diplomatic, economic, and propaganda weapons. It has not led to a direct military clash between the principal opponents, the United States and the Soviet Union.

The War Years

During the war years, U.S. policy was based on getting along with the Soviet Union at almost any price. This was partly due to military necessity. The Soviet army was keeping most of the German forces busy on the Eastern front. Moreover, some American military leaders wanted Soviet help in the war against Japan. As events were to prove, Japan's military strength by 1945 was much overrated. Also, the later invasion of Manchuria and North Korea by the Soviets was of no particular help to the United States in defeating Japan, but served rather to advance the political aims of the Communists.

The American people, by and large, recognized the military value of their government's close cooperation with and assistance to the Soviet government. However, many Americans who admired the Soviet people's heroic stand against the Germans transferred this feeling of admiration to one of sympathy for the Communist system itself.

After the war, as the Soviet Union crushed the hopes of freedom in one nation after another in Eastern Europe and the Balkans, there was a reawakening among Americans to the real nature of communism. The Soviet Union's violation of the agreement made at Yalta to conduct free elections in the nations freed from Germany's control was one of the first causes of the shift from wartime alliance to cold war.

The Soviet government followed a pattern that was repeated in country after country, wherever Soviet troops were in occupation at the end of the war. At first there would be a so-called anti-fascist coalition government, in which liberals and Socialists would be included along with Communists. The Communists always kept control of two departments: the ministry of the interior, which meant they could control the police; and the ministry of education, which allowed them to inject their propaganda into the schools.

The Soviet Satellites

Within a few years, a bloc of Soviet satellite countries grew up in the part of Europe that had not been occupied by American and British troops.

COMMUNISM EXPANDS IN EUROPE

NORWAY

North Sea

SWEDEN

DENMARK

Baltic Sea

FINLAND 1944

ESTONIA 1940

LATVIA 1940

LITHUANIA 1940

Berlin

EAST GERMANY 1945

WEST GERMANY

POLAND 1947

S O V I E T

R U S S I A

CZECHOSLOVAKIA 1948

① AUSTRIA

HUNGARY 1947

ITALY

ROMANIA 1946

YUGOSLAVIA 1945

Adriatic Sea

Black Sea

BULGARIA 1946

0 50 100 150 200
Statute Miles

ALBANIA 1946

TURKEY

GREECE

TURKEY

Soviet Russia before 1939

|||||||||| Acquired by Soviet Russia During World War II

Nations Taken Over by Communists After World War II

① Eastern Austria was occupied by Soviet Russia from 1945 to 1955

One of the satellites, Czechoslovakia, for a time maintained a show of democratic institutions in its coalition government. However, it followed Moscow's lead in all matters of foreign policy. It renounced aid under the Marshall Plan (see page 181) when so instructed by Stalin, and always voted with the Soviet Union in the United Nations.

But even this was not enough for Moscow's purposes. In February, 1948, the Czechoslovak Communists, who were well represented in the coalition government, brought off a bloodless *coup* in Prague, and Czechoslovakia was drawn completely behind what became known as the "Iron Curtain."

The Partition of Germany

Along with the division of Europe into Communist-ruled and non-Communist sections, there was an informal partition of Germany. According to the Potsdam Agreement of August, 1945, occupied Germany was to be treated as a single economic unit and democratic political parties were to be encouraged. Meanwhile the country was divided into four zones of occupation, each to be administered by one of the four major Allies. The Soviet Zone consisted of the eastern part of Germany up to a line along the River Elbe and as far south as the northern frontier of Bavaria. The American Zone included Bavaria and parts of southern and western Germany, with the important cities of Frankfurt and Stuttgart. The British took over northwestern Germany, with the industrial Ruhr and Rhineland area and the big port of Hamburg. The French were given a smaller zone in southwestern Germany.

The division extended to the city of Berlin, the former German capital. Berlin, too, was divided into four sectors. About 2,200,000 people lived under free institutions in the three Western sectors. About 1,500,000 lived in the Soviet sector, which was ruled by Communist methods. Movement within Berlin was fairly free until the Soviets encircled East

DIVIDED GERMANY

North Sea

Baltic Sea

DENMARK

Hamburg

NETHERLANDS

Hanover

Berlin

POLAND

Brussels

EAST GERMANY

BELGIUM

Bonn

LUXEMBOURG

Frankfurt

Prague

CZECHOSLOVAKIA

WEST GERMANY

FRANCE

Stuttgart

Munich

Vienna

AUSTRIA

Bern

SWITZERLAND

| 0 | 25 | 50 | 75 | 100 |

Statute Miles

MAJOR ROUTES BETWEEN WEST GERMANY AND WEST BERLIN

Air Corridors
Railroads
Highways
Canals
Under Communist Control

DIVIDED BERLIN

French Zone

Russian Zone

British Zone

U.S. Zone

| 0 | 5 | 10 | Statute Miles |

Berlin with a wall in August, 1961, in order to stop the tremendous outflow of refugees from East Berlin to West Berlin (see page 79).

The Russians had captured Berlin in May, 1945. Since the city was surrounded on all sides by the agreed-upon Soviet Zone of Occupation, it was necessary for the Western Allies to negotiate with the Russians regarding access to Berlin. During the fighting, American troops had advanced some distance into the future Soviet Zone. General Lucius D. Clay, acting on instructions from General Eisenhower, agreed with the Russians that Americans should enter their sector of Berlin more or less simultaneously with the withdrawal of American forces from the Soviet Zone.

In his memoirs, General Clay expresses regret that he did not make free access to Berlin a condition for the withdrawal of the American troops. At that time, however, hope of preserving friendship with the Soviet government was still strong. Clay settled for the assignment to Allied use of a main highway, a railway, and three air corridors as a "temporary" arrangement. In addition to the five military routes, there is limited civilian access to West Berlin from West Germany via rail, canal, and highway (see map on page 61).

Resistance in Berlin

The Western position in Berlin was first challenged in June, 1948. Stalin used as an excuse for this action the decision of the Western Allies to issue new money in West Germany and West Berlin, in a move to support the falling Deutschmark. The Soviets protested bitterly and closed rail, road, and canal access to the city. Apparently the Soviets expected that the resulting hardships to the people would force a withdrawal of the Western forces from the city, and that Berlin would then become the capital of a Sovietized East Germany.

West Berlin was saved without a direct armed showdown by a gigantic airlift which carried fuel, foodstuffs, and other

During the Soviet blockade of Berlin, U.S. and British planes
air-lifted millions of tons of supplies to besieged citizens.

supplies into the city. By early 1949 this airlift was bringing
in 8,000 tons of supplies a day, an amount equal to that
formerly transported by rail and highway. Furthermore, a
counterblockade against exports of West German steel and
coal to the Soviet Zone of Germany was making itself felt
in East Germany. In the spring of 1949 the Soviet Union
called off its blockade. Despite minor clashes and harass-
ments, the status of the city was not seriously challenged for
nine years, until Soviet Premier Khrushchev, in November,

63

1958, launched an on-again, off-again crisis that was intensified in 1961 (see Chapter 6).

While the Soviet Union was tightening its grip on its satellite empire, stamping out the last remains of political independence, the United States had not been idle. In the spring of 1946, Secretary of State James F. Byrnes and the ranking Republican in the Senate Foreign Affairs Committee, Arthur Vandenberg, delivered strongly worded speeches on the necessity of opposing further Soviet aggression.

A significant landmark was President Harry S. Truman's message to Congress on March 12, 1947, asking for an appropriation of $400,000,000 for aid to Greece and Turkey. Commenting on the dire consequences faced by the United States, President Truman stated:

> Totalitarian regimes imposed on free peoples, by direct or indirect aggression, undermine foundations of international peace and hence the security of the United States.

The Soviet Union then turned on Turkey and Greece. In Turkey the offense was a diplomatic one. The Soviet government threatened to take over the defense of the Dardanelles (a goal which Molotov had tried to achieve in his talks with the Nazis in 1940). The government-controlled Soviet press also demanded the cession to the Soviet Union of the Turkish northeastern provinces of Kars and Ardahan. The Turks stood firm, with U.S. encouragement, and the Soviets backed down short of war.

In Greece, Communists were waging a devastating civil war with arms supplied by the adjacent Communist-ruled countries of Bulgaria and Yugoslavia. The United States helped the Greek government put down the rebels by sending military and economic aid and by ordering the U.S. Sixth Fleet into the Mediterranean. This show of force convinced Stalin that the United States meant business. He persuaded an unwilling Tito to bring the civil war to an end.

A contributing factor in the defeat of the Greek Communists was the breach between Marshal Tito's Communist dictatorship in Yugoslavia and the hierarchy in Moscow in 1948. The principal cause of this breach was Stalin's demand for a degree of direct Soviet control over Yugoslavia's internal affairs, which Tito rejected. For several years, until the death of Stalin in 1953, the Soviet government attempted, by all methods short of actual war, to overthrow Tito. It enforced an economic boycott and incited attacks by satellite states bordering on Yugoslavia. (There is no common frontier between the Soviet Union and Yugoslavia, which made it easier for Tito to assert his independence.) American military and economic help was sent to Yugoslavia, and Tito closed his border to the Greek guerrillas.

The Korean War

When the Communists finally seized power in mainland China (see Chapter 10), the Nationalist government fled to the island of Taiwan (Formosa), which became its stronghold. Soon a grave challenge to international peace appeared in the neighboring peninsula of Korea. This former possession of Japan was arbitrarily divided, along the line of the 38th parallel, into areas of occupation by the Soviet Union in the north and the United States in the south. The Soviet occupation forces blocked all efforts to reunite the two halves of the country. In 1948 they refused to permit U.N. supervision of elections in North Korea and set up an independent republic (the People's Democratic Republic of Korea). In South Korea the election was held and the veteran Korean Nationalist Syngman Rhee was elected President of the Republic of Korea. He officially maintained parliamentary institutions (which were not always fully observed in spirit) and a free economic system.

The Soviet Union built up North Korean military power and withdrew in 1948, leaving a well-equipped army of peas-

American infantrymen "mopping up" through burning shacks of Sukchon, Korea, after a U.N. attack late in the Korean War.

ants and workers. In South Korea, the United States concentrated on economic aid. When American troops withdrew in 1949, they left only a lightly armed Korean military force for police actions and border patrol. On June 25, 1950, the North Korean army crossed the 38th parallel in force. At first the Reds swept all before them, in spite of the American military intervention which was ordered by President Truman with the authorization of the U.N. Security Council. Unanimous approval in this body was made possible only by the fact that the Soviet Union had "walked out" of the Security Council in a huff a short time before, over the question of permitting the Communist rather than the Nationalist government to represent China in the United Nations.

Other members of the United Nations, including Great Britain, France, Turkey, Greece, and the Philippines, sent small military units to Korea. But the brunt of the fighting fell to the South Korean and American forces. The war was marked by swift shifts of fortune. At first the South Korean and American troops were confined to a narrow perimeter around the southern port of Pusan. General Douglas MacArthur's successful landing at Inchon in September, 1950, led to the encirclement and rout of the North Koreans, the recapture of Seoul, the capital, and a successful advance into North Korea.

Just when all appeared to be going well for South Korea, massive Red Chinese intervention (in November) changed the picture, and the U.N. troops were driven south to the 38th parallel. There was some recovery, and Seoul, which had fallen into the hands of the Reds a second time, was retaken. A speech by the Soviet U.N. delegate, Jacob Malik, hinting that the Reds would be willing to end the fighting along the then established battle lines, led to a reduction of military activity on both sides in the summer of 1951.

Conclusion of a formal armistice was long delayed because of Communist insistence that all prisoners of war be returned. While only a handful of American prisoners chose to remain in Red China (and most of these subsequently returned home), the majority of North Korean and Chinese prisoners in the hands of the U.N. forces did not wish to return to their Communist-ruled homelands.

Pressure was eased by the death of Joseph Stalin on March 5, 1953, and the prisoners were given freedom of choice. Most of the North Koreans stayed in South Korea and about three fourths of the Chinese decided to go to Taiwan. The armistice, signed in the summer of 1953, ended a war which had cost U.N. forces more than 150,000 casualties.

Though a new leadership was in control in the Kremlin, the Cold War went on unabated.

CHAPTER 5 — STUDY AIDS

Words and Names to Understand

puppet government	bloc	economic boycott
coalition government	Iron Curtain	U.N. Security Council

Checkup Questions

1. What actions by the Soviet Union after the war made Americans aware of the real nature of communism?
2. How did the Soviet government gain control over the satellite states?
3. How was Germany divided geographically after the war? What nations controlled the zones of occupation?
4. What steps did the United States take to halt Soviet expansion in Europe after the war?
5. Why was it so difficult to bring about an armistice in the Korean War?

Questions to Think About

1. How have political, diplomatic, economic, and propaganda weapons been used in the Cold War?
2. Why did the Soviets want to force the Western nations to withdraw from Berlin?
3. Why is economic boycott an effective weapon in the Cold War?

Books, Pamphlets, and Articles to Read

Paperback Books:

Seton-Watson, Hugh, *From Lenin to Khrushchev.* Praeger, 1960; Chs. 12 and 13.

Roberts, Henry L., *Russia and America.* Mentor, 1956; Ch. 9.

The Soviet Union, Scholastic Book Services, 1962, 1963; Chs. 9, 10.

Other Books:

Berger, Carl, *The Korea Knot.* University of Pennsylvania Press, 1957.

Djilas, Milovan, *Conversations with Stalin.* Harcourt, Brace, 1962.

Clay, Lucius P., *Decision in Germany.* Doubleday, 1950.

Articles:

"Along the Iron Curtain." *Look,* Jan. 30, 1962.

"Berlin: Summer, 1961." *Atlas,* Sept., 1961.

"We Can Now Make a Deal on Berlin," Charles W. Thayer. *Harper's,* June, 1962.

Coexistence with Khrushchev

Joseph Stalin, the dreaded dictator of the Soviet Union who had sent so many others to their deaths, died on March 5, 1953, under rather mysterious circumstances. He was 73 years old.

Did Stalin die a natural death, as officially reported, or was he finished off by highly placed lieutenants who feared their own destruction? Those who might cast some light on the matter have either vanished or dare not speak out so long as they remain in the U.S.S.R.

Who was to inherit Stalin's power? Under the Soviet system, there was no constitutionally designated successor; nor was there any machinery for holding a free election. The immediate sequel to Stalin's death was the assumption of power by a group of three: Georgi Malenkov, an influential Stalin lieutenant; Vyacheslav Molotov, one of the "old guard," who had served as Premier and Foreign Minister under Stalin; and Lavrenti Beria, a Georgian, like Stalin, who had headed the secret police since 1939.

At first it seemed that Malenkov had inherited Stalin's power. An efficient administrator, the young man of Cossack origin rose under Stalin to high government posts. He now held the offices of Premier and First Secretary of the Communist Party. But six months after Stalin's death in September, 1953, he relinquished the Party post to Nikita Khrushchev, a comrade who had also been a high Party functionary under Stalin. This crafty peasant from the province of Kursk had been a mechanic before joining the Revolution at the age of 23. He became a Party member in 1918 and was educated in a Party school at Kharkov University. Khrushchev's work in the Moscow Communist organization and his zeal in carrying out the purges during the collectivization program in the Ukraine won Stalin's favor.

Although Khrushchev had done nothing to oppose the ruthless arrests and persecutions when Stalin was still alive, he soon joined with others in a program designed to downgrade Stalin.

Reaction against Stalin

The "doctor's plot"* was publicly declared to be a fraud and an injustice to innocent men. Many persons who had survived imprisonment and torture were set free. There was wide-scale release of prisoners in forced-labor camps and reduction of sentences of others. There was talk of instituting "Socialist legality" — a sort of rule by law. Whereas Stalin had kept rigidly aloof from social contacts with foreigners, the new Soviet rulers began to appear at embassy parties. They took up residence outside the Kremlin, the great fortress-palace in which Stalin had maintained his headquarters and had kept his closest colleagues under vigilant control.

---

*In January, 1953, nine leading doctors of the Soviet Union, six or seven of whom were Jewish, were arrested on the basis of false accusations that they had plotted the murder of Party leaders and high army officers.

In foreign relations, tensions lessened too. Stalin's death was followed by the 1953 armistice in Korea. In 1955 Khrushchev and other Soviet leaders went to Belgrade to patch up relations with Tito's Yugoslavia.

Soon after the visit to Belgrade, the Soviet government consented to sign a peace treaty with Austria on condition that it become a neutral state. Both Soviet and Western occupation troops were withdrawn and Austria's independence was restored.

Internal Rivalries

While the Soviet Union was cementing friendships abroad, the home front bristled with rivalries. Although the country was now supposedly ruled by a group of leaders (instead of one individual), conflicts continued behind the scenes. The first open break in the unity of the new bosses came with the arrest of Lavrenti Beria on June 26, 1953. According to the official version, Beria was executed after a secret trial some months later. It is still not known what led to his downfall. Possibly his powerful political police organization, with its special military units and powers of investigation, arrest, and punishment by secret courts, had become such a state within a state that the new Soviet rulers felt uncomfortable in its shadow.

A number of Beria's henchmen were also executed, but in general there has been a difference between Khrushchev's rise to supreme power and Stalin's. Except in the case of Beria, Khrushchev's defeated rivals have been demoted, not killed.

The next milestone on Khrushchev's road to power was the ouster of Malenkov as Premier in February of 1955. One theory about Malenkov's displacement is that he had a difference of opinion with the military leadership over converting more of industry to consumer goods. This seemed to threaten the priority given to "heavy" industries producing

WIDE WORLD

Malenkov, Khrushchev, and Bulganin were still congenial in 1954, shortly before Malenkov's ouster as Premier. Khrushchev removed Bulganin, Malenkov's successor, three years later.

machines and war equipment. After the fall of Malenkov, Nikolai Bulganin became Premier, while the ever more powerful Khrushchev, as First Secretary, tightened his grip on the Communist Party.

It is a measure of the terror which the very memory of Stalin inspired that almost three years elapsed after his death before there was any effort to challenge publicly the myth that he had been an all-wise, all-benevolent "father of the Soviet peoples." To be sure, the chorus of praise that was heaped on Stalin during his life came to an abrupt end. His name was rarely mentioned in newspapers or speeches. However, he was posthumously honored by having his embalmed body placed beside that of Lenin in the mausoleum in Red Square in Moscow.

Khrushchev Downgrades Stalin

At the 20th Congress of the Communist Party in 1956 the veteran Soviet trade minister, Anastas Mikoyan, broke the ice by voicing criticisms of Stalin. These paled by comparison with the revelations that Khrushchev made to a closed session of the Congress. This speech by Khrushchev has never been published in the Soviet Union, but the substance of what he said filtered out to foreign countries.

Khrushchev stressed the crimes that Stalin had committed against Communist Party members during the purges of the 1930's. It was not until 1961, however, that Khrushchev's attack on Stalin reached its final stage, with further denunciations at the 22nd Party Congress, and the removal of Stalin's body from the showcase tomb to burial in an ordinary grave. Khrushchev said enough, however, to arouse considerable disillusionment, especially in foreign Communist parties. This was a factor, although not the only one, in the unrest that spread through the Soviet satellites in 1956.

The Poznan Riots

In June, in the Polish city of Poznan, a strike against a food shortage and low wages turned into a riot. Troops were called out and blood was shed. Forty-four of the rioters were killed, hundreds wounded. One thousand arrests were made. By October the dissatisfaction, even among the local Party members, had swelled to the point where the Poles demanded the return to power of Wladyslaw Gomulka. Gomulka was a Polish Communist leader who had been imprisoned because he wanted the Polish regime to be run by native Communists rather than by officials from Moscow and their local stooges. Khrushchev himself rushed to Warsaw with prominent Soviet leaders and ordered an alert to Soviet troops in Poland. Gomulka was restored to power and an armed revolt was avoided.

A truckload of freedom fighters moves into position outside Budapest, just before Soviet heavy artillery was called in to help crush the Hungarian rebellion in November, 1956.

Communist leadership in Poland won a large measure of independence. War Minister Konstantin Rokossovsky and other Soviet citizens in top positions in Poland were recalled to the Soviet Union. The Polish people were somewhat pacified by the release from house arrest of their spiritual leader, Cardinal Wyszynski. Peasants were permitted to withdraw from the collectives and set up their own farms again. The power of the secret police was curbed. Freedoms of speech and the press were temporarily broadened, as a concession to intellectuals and students. The price paid by the Polish leaders for this milder form of communism was complete cooperation with the U.S.S.R. in matters of foreign policy and international Communist activity.

The Hungarian Revolt

Developments in Hungary were much more serious and tragic. A spontaneous uprising of students and workers broke out in Budapest on October 23, 1956, and spread rapidly throughout the country. A new regime — still proclaiming Socialist aims, but pledged to restore democratic liberties and a multiparty system of government — began to take shape under the leadership of Imre Nagy, a veteran Hungarian Communist. Like Gomulka in Poland, he had been imprisoned for his efforts in behalf of national independence. Cardinal Mindszenty and other political prisoners were released. The hated secret police were hunted down.

For a few days the Soviet government took no action. It probably hoped that concessions to local self-rule would keep Hungary, like Poland, in the Soviet bloc. But when Nagy withdrew from the Warsaw Pact — a military alliance of Communist countries (see page 146) — and appealed to the United Nations to support Hungary's position as a neutral nation, Khrushchev decided to strike. His killing blow was masked by treachery. The Soviets pretended to remove their troops from Hungary, in line with Nagy's request, and invited Pal Maleter and other Hungarian military leaders to a conference, ostensibly to discuss details of the Soviet military withdrawal. The Hungarian commanders never returned from this conference. On November 4 the Soviet forces, under cover of heavy artillery fire, launched a massive attack on Budapest. Resistance was crushed. Nagy, who had taken refuge in the Yugoslav Embassy, was lured out by a safe-conduct pass and arrested on the spot by Soviet police. Neither Nagy nor Maleter was seen again. Their execution was announced in 1958.

A new puppet government, acceptable to Khrushchev, was set up under Janos Kadar, a Communist once associated with Nagy. Protests and resolutions of censure in the United Nations were ignored by the Soviet government. The brief days of freedom in Hungary were over.

Khrushchev Becomes Dictator

The year 1957 was for Khrushchev a year of crisis and of triumph. His new policies were unpopular. Resistance was growing to his scheme for decentralizing the top-heavy management of industry and developing uncultivated lands in Siberia and Central Asia. This reaction was stimulated by unrest in the Soviet satellite states. Khrushchev actually found himself outvoted at a session of the Presidium, the inner steering committee of the Communist Party, in June, 1957. His opponents were a coalition of old Stalinists — including Molotov, Kaganovich, and partisans of Malenkov — who wanted to cut down the military buildup in order to produce more consumer goods.

Khrushchev, however, appealed from the Presidium to the larger Central Committee, which he had filled with his own men. The Central Committee upheld Khrushchev, and his opponents were expelled from the Presidium. There is evidence that Khrushchev owed his success partly to the support of Marshal Georgi Zhukov, one of the outstanding Soviet military leaders in World War II. Stalin, suspecting Zhukov of disloyalty, had banished him from the government. But after Stalin's death, Zhukov became Minister of Defense and was back in the inner circle of the Communist ruling group. Eventually Khrushchev, fearing that Zhukov was challenging his leadership, ousted the unsuspecting Marshal from his post while he was traveling in the Balkans.

The Berlin Dispute

On November 27, 1958, the new Soviet dictator made his first move to expel the Western powers from West Berlin, which they had occupied since 1945. Since then this drive has been intensified at times, relaxed at others. West Berlin has a free and prosperous economy, and is protected by American, British, and French troops. To the West Berliners, the presence of these troops is a guarantee against any attempt by the Soviet Union or by its East German Communist leaders to take away their freedom. Free elections, in which Communists were allowed to participate, have shown that over 98 per cent of the people of West Berlin are opposed to communism — the effects of which they can see at first hand in East Berlin.

Since 1958, Khrushchev has proposed repeatedly that West Berlin be turned into a "demilitarized free city," with all Western troops withdrawn. He announced his intention to sign a peace treaty with the "German Democratic Republic," the Communist-ruled regime which has been imposed on the part of Germany under Soviet occupation. Khrushchev declared that his signing of this treaty would mean the end of American, British, and French rights of access to West Berlin, unless the West negotiated new rights with the German Democratic Republic. (That regime is diplomatically recognized by Communist-ruled countries.)

Khrushchev at first set a six-month deadline for the meeting of his demands. However, he dropped this time limit when the Western powers agreed to meet the Soviet Union in a conference at Geneva. Although the conference of foreign ministers led to no positive results, Khrushchev later visited the United States at President Eisenhower's invitation; and a "summit conference" of heads of state of the Soviet Union and the three Western powers was set for mid-May, 1960, in Paris. This meeting never was completed, be-

SOVFOTO

Khrushchev studies remains of downed American U-2 plane.
Its flight was his pretext for halting 1960 summit meeting.

cause of Khrushchev's demand that President Eisenhower
apologize for an incident involving an American U-2 plane.
This plane, on a reconnaissance mission, was brought down
while flying over the Soviet Union. Although Khrushchev
indulged in abusive tirades when President Eisenhower refused to issue an apology, Khrushchev took no further action
against West Berlin until after the U.S. presidential election
that fall.

The Berlin dispute became acute again in June, 1961, during a brief meeting between President Kennedy and Premier Khrushchev in Vienna. Khrushchev insisted on a settlement of the Berlin issue by the end of 1961, and repeated his threat to sign a peace treaty with his puppet regime in East Germany if this ultimatum were not met. President Kennedy announced America's determination to stand by its obligations to defend the freedom and independence of West Berlin; he called up reserves, sent replacements to Europe, and made other military preparations.

A striking and ominous change took place in the status of Berlin on August 13, when the Communist authorities

East Berlin masons work on the 25-mile wall, built by Reds in 1961 to keep East Germans from fleeing to West Berlin.

began building a wall, separating East Berlin from West Berlin. The purpose of the wall was to prevent a continuation of the mass flight of Germans from the Communist-ruled Soviet Zone to West Berlin, and thence to West Germany. This wall violated the four-power agreements of 1945 and 1949, which had promised freedom of movement within the entire city. The United States reinforced its garrison in Berlin, and there were occasional shooting incidents as East Germans continued to try to escape.

In October, Khrushchev called off his December 31 deadline for the signing of a Berlin treaty with East German authorities. But as months passed, the U.S.S.R. and the Western powers remained as far apart as ever on acceptable terms for a Berlin settlement. There were various complications. During this period the East Berlin authorities for a time renewed an old practice of sending military planes into the air corridors to harass Allied commercial flights to and from Berlin. Although this activity was annoying to Western pilots, it did not result in any loss of life or property damage.

The Arms Deadlock

On another issue, there was also complete disagreement between the United States and the Soviet Union. This was the limitation of armaments. A number of conferences had been held since 1958 on the question of disarmament. No concrete results were reached because of one overriding deadlock. The United States and the other Western powers maintained that disarmament could not succeed without an international system of inspection and control. The Soviet Union, while professing to favor sweeping disarmament, refused to permit inspections by any international group on Soviet soil.

At one time, success seemed possible in one phase of armament control: the testing of nuclear weapons. A conference between representatives of the three main nuclear

Premier Khrushchev looks on as (l. to r.) U.S. Secretary of State Dean Rusk, Soviet Foreign Minister Andrei Gromyko, and British Prime Minister Sir Alec Douglas-Home sign limited nuclear test-ban treaty in the Kremlin, August 5, 1963.

powers — the United States, Great Britain, and the Soviet Union — went on for almost three years in Geneva. Nuclear tests were suspended by the participants, presumably for the duration of the conferences.

Then, on August 30, 1961, the Soviet government violated the moratorium and for several weeks carried on open-air tests. Some of the devices set off by the U.S.S.R. in this series of tests were of very high explosive power. After having tested the biggest bomb ever detonated, Moscow proposed that the major powers again accept an uninspected suspension of tests.

On April 25, 1962, the United States, with the backing of Britain, started a new series of atmospheric tests near Christmas Island in the Pacific.

President Kennedy announced that the United States was reluctant to resume nuclear testing but that, in the absence of a policed test ban, the tests were necessary for the security of the Western powers. The United States, he said, would make every effort to reach agreement with the Soviet Union to end nuclear tests. For use in time of emergency, the United States and the Soviet Union agreed in June, 1963, to set up a direct communications link (the "hot line"). In August, 1963, a limited treaty, banning nuclear tests in the atmosphere, in outer space, and under water, was concluded, and in October it was agreed in principle to ban nuclear weapons from space vehicles in orbit. President Johnson moved swiftly after President Kennedy's assassination to assure Khrushchev he would continue the policy of seeking better relations with the Soviet Union.

Crises in the Congo and Cuba

In mid-1960 a major crisis broke out in the new Republic of the Congo. The establishment of this independent state with insufficient preparation for self-rule threatened to embroil the Soviet Union and the Western powers in armed conflict when an internal struggle for power broke out. The Soviets supported Congo Premier Patrice Lumumba, who sought a strong central government. Congo President Joseph Kasavubu, friendly to the West, sought a loose federation of states. The U.N. rushed in a 20,000-man army to restore order. U.N. Secretary General Dag Hammarskjold flew to the Congo in September, 1961, to arrange a cease-fire, only to die there in a plane crash. The Congo drifted between peace and war until January, 1963, when U.N. efforts appeared successful in stabilizing the situation.

Even more dangerous was the threat of direct confrontation of Soviet and American military force when in October, 1962, President Kennedy exposed the presence of offensive Soviet missiles in Cuba. After a week of extreme tension, the Soviets agreed to dismantle the missile bases, but some Soviet troops remained in Cuba (*see Chapter 7*).

CHAPTER 6 — STUDY AIDS

Words and Names to Understand

"Socialist legality"   "demilitarized free city"   *troika*

Checkup Questions

1. What three men assumed power after Stalin died?
2. What changes in foreign policy were made by Khrushchev after Stalin's death?
3. What effect did Khrushchev's attack on Stalin during the 20th Congress have on the Soviet satellite states?
4. Describe the revolt against Communist rule in Hungary; in Poland.
5. Why did the "summit conference" in 1960 fail?

Questions to Think About

1. Why was there no provision under the Soviet system for a successor to Joseph Stalin?
2. Why has Khrushchev tried to downgrade Stalin and change his policies?
3. Why does the Soviet Union remain a U.N. member when it seems to have so much contempt for its resolutions and policies?
4. What are the major issues on which the United States and the Soviet Union are deadlocked?

Books, Pamphlets, and Articles to Read

Paperback Books:

Brumberg, Abraham, ed., *Russia under Khrushchev.* Praeger, 1962; pp. 71-126.

Rostow, W. W., *The Dynamics of Soviet Society.* Mentor, 1954; Ch. 15.

Schwartz, Harry, ed., *The Many Faces of Communism.* Berkley, 1962; Ch. 14.

Other Books:

Gunther, John, *Inside Russia Today.* Harper, 1962; Chs. 11 and 12.

Articles:

"Dissension Inside the Kremlin," Edward Crankshaw. *The Atlantic,* June, 1962.

"Five Clues to the Khrushchev Riddle," James H. Billington. *New York Times Magazine,* Oct. 29, 1961.

"The Problem of Coexistence," Alvin Z. Rubinstein. *Current History,* Nov., 1961.

7

The Many Shades of Communism

There are shades of communism — variations in the way the Communist system is operated. There is the Khrushchev shade in the Soviet Union, the Mao shade in continental China, the Tito shade in Yugoslavia. But whatever the shade, all hold fast to a system that makes the individual subservient to the all-powerful state, that denies him civil rights and freedom of choice, that deprives him of the sense of human dignity that is his right as a human being.

So, in tracing the changes that have taken place in the Communist governments as their leaders tried this and that means of securing their power, one should keep in mind that the essence of communism is what it has been all along: a tyranny over the people.

Early "Heresies"

Despite rigid Party discipline, there have been many disagreements among Russian Communists. One early disagreement, which affected the course of events after Lenin's death, arose between Lenin and Trotsky. It dealt with the development of the Communist Revolution. Both Lenin and Trotsky were in a way trying to revise the timetable set up by their supreme teacher, Marx. Marx believed that the change to communism in a society could not take place until capitalism had reached a high state of development. Then and only then could the workers take over the vast system of efficient factories and productive lands, and proceed to establish a society along Socialist (or Communist) lines. (Marx used the terms "Socialist" and "Communist" interchangeably.)

Capitalism in Russia in 1917 was still in a very early stage of development. There had been progress in the building of railroads and in manufacturing and mining, but a long period of capitalist growth seemed necessary before the country was ripe for a Communist revolution. During this period, according to the theories of Marx, the "bourgeoisie," or propertied classes, would control the government.

Lenin, however, was eager to get on with the revolution. So he skirted this difficulty by proposing a "dictatorship of the proletariat." In this way he expected to skip the period of building up the economy under a capitalist system, which Marx said was necessary.

Trotsky agreed with Lenin that, once the Tsar was overthrown, a sweeping revolution would push aside the weak Russian middle class and bring a group of revolutionary Socialists into power. But Trotsky foresaw a stumbling block: the peasantry. Trotsky was convinced that the new order would collapse because of the strong desire of the peasants to preserve their private property. The only thing that could assure the success of a Communist revolution in Russia, he believed, was a Communist revolution in countries that were industrially more advanced than Russia. This theory of "permanent revolution" became known as "Trotskyism," and created splits in the Communist movement throughout the world. Trotskyism declined, however, after its leader's murder in Mexico in 1940 by a Stalin agent (see Chapter 3). Today it is limited to a few small groups.

Later "Heresies"

Later there were more disagreements within the ranks of the Russian Communist Party. The Bolshevik ideal of equality suffered a severe setback once the Bolsheviks had seized power in Russia. There were wide variations in the standard of living of Party leaders and Party-appointed factory and farm managers on the one hand, and the average worker or peasant on the other. This caused many discontented groups to spring up within the Party.

One of these was the Workers' Opposition movement. It developed within the ranks of the Communist Party during the years of war communism (see Chapter 3). Its platform called for more participation by workers in the management of the factories, a reform of the inefficient bureaucracy, and an end to special favors for the Communists.

In 1921 all factions within the Party were forbidden. Although the Workers' Opposition was disbanded, its tradition persisted in such small splinter organizations as the Workers' Group, headed by Gabriel Myasnikov, a factory worker; and the Workers' Truth, led by an old Bolshevik named Bogdanov. Myasnikov's group was harassed out of existence by the secret police. The Bogdanov movement also withered on the vine. Its theoretical position is interesting, however, because it strikingly foreshadowed the stand taken some 40 years later by the Yugoslav Communist Milovan Djilas, a stand for which he was jailed:

> The Communist Party . . . after becoming the ruling party of the organizers and leaders of the state apparatus and of the capitalist-based economic life . . . irrevocably lost its tie and community with the proletariat.

Milovan Djilas, former Vice-President of Yugoslavia and one of the top Yugoslav Party officials, was stripped of all his posts and imprisoned several times for daring to criticize the Communist system.

So thorough and ruthless were Stalin's purges in the 1930's of real or imagined "heretics" that even since his death there has been no convincing evidence of organized political opposition to communism within the Party. Today, speech has become a little freer and notes of criticism have penetrated a few novels and poems, but there seems to be no opposition group in the Soviet Union with a clearly defined program. It is in the international Communist movement that differing shades appear in theory and action.

Tito's "Deviation"

The first big break in the ironclad unity of international communism was the refusal of the Yugoslav dictator, Josip Broz Tito, to accept Soviet dictation of Yugoslavia's internal affairs. This led to an open breach between Tito and Stalin in 1948. Since then, Yugoslavia has remained a Communist dictatorship, with a solidly Communist controlled economic system.

Yugoslavia has developed certain independent features in its economic system. Instead of having the state run the whole economy directly, workers' councils were set up in factories, offices, and stores. Peasants were allowed to withdraw from collective farms, and 90 per cent of them did. Perhaps the most distinctive characteristic of Yugoslavia, after the break with Moscow, was its insistence that every country should find its own way to socialism.

While remaining a dictatorship run by Communist methods and with ultimate Communist goals, Yugoslavia has retained its national independence. The Yugoslav brand of communism, unlike the Soviet and Chinese brands, does not seem to be pursuing aggressive or imperialist aims.

From 1962 on there have been signs of increasing cordiality and cooperation between the Soviet Union and Yugoslavia. For the first time since 1948, Yugoslavia has received military equipment, such as heavy tanks, from the Soviet Union. On issues of the Cold War, Tito has been on the Soviet side more often than on the American.

As Tito was a rebel and "heretic," from the standpoint of Stalinism, so Tito's second in command, Milovan Djilas, became a "heretic" to Tito. Djilas was expelled from the government and the Party in 1954 for criticizing the conduct of his fellow Communist leaders in Yugoslavia. Since then he has been arrested and imprisoned several times because of his books and articles critical of communism.

Tito maintained that Moscow should not dictate the policies of national Communist parties and that the Soviet Union should not interfere in the internal affairs of other Communist-ruled nations.

Djilas carried this reasoning further and argued with force and clarity, in his book *The New Class,* that communism itself, installed in power, was a new system of privilege and oppression. Writes Djilas:

Power is an end in itself and the essence of contemporary communism. Power is almost exclusively an end in communism, because it is both the source and the guaranty of all privileges. By means of and through power the material privileges and ownership of the ruling class over national goods are realized. . . . With the victory of a Communist revolution in a country a new class comes into power and into control.

Centers of Communism

Moscow is no longer the sole center of international communism. Communist China represents a second center (see Chapter 10) — a potent rival of Moscow. Yugoslavia is a nationalistic expression of communism. Still a fourth center is Castro's Cuba. Castro sees himself as the leader of communism in Latin America. Though ideologically he is closer to the Mao brand of communism, Castro depends heavily on Soviet economic and military aid. This tends to modify somewhat his militancy.

In October, 1962, U.S. reconnaissance planes discovered that the Soviets had installed offensive ballistic missiles in Cuba. The U.S. took quick and dramatic action. President Kennedy ordered a sea and air quarantine on shipments of arms to Cuba. The United States was prepared to risk war to prevent the delivery of offensive weapons to the island. President Kennedy branded as a lie the Soviet statement that missiles with a range of 1,100 to 2,200 miles were defensive. He demanded that the Soviet Union dismantle the launching sites and withdraw the missiles, bombers, and personnel.

The Soviet Union backed down. They shipped the missiles and bombers back and proceeded to dismantle the launching sites.

This was a critical moment in U. S. history. As Secretary of State Dean Rusk expressed it, "We stood eyeball to eyeball, and I think the other fellow just blinked." Standing by the United States were the Organization of American States, European and Asiatic allies, and many neutral states.

Cuba today is still in the business of exporting revolution to Latin America with the assistance of Communist China. The Chinese Communists criticized Khrushchev for withdrawing from Cuba. They told him that the United States was only a "paper tiger." Khrushchev replied that the "paper tiger" had "atomic teeth."

Cuba's Premier Fidel Castro appears to be in a good humor as he chats affably with Soviet Premier Nikita Khrushchev (left) during a visit to the U.S.S.R. in January, 1964.

However they may differ among themselves with regard to emphasis and detail, all Communist governments deny political and personal liberties to the people who live under them. While in some Communist countries the individual is more strictly controlled than in others, all forms of communism stress the theory that the individual is made for the state, not the state for the individual. All, except the Yugoslav regime for the time being, are bent on aggressive expansion through propaganda, infiltration, and subversion. All are hostile to the United States and to the survival of free institutions for which America and the other democratic nations stand.

CHAPTER 7 — STUDY AIDS

Words and Names to Understand

heretics   Trotskyism   imperialist

Checkup Questions

1. How did Lenin propose to bypass the period of capitalism Marx felt was necessary?
2. What did Trotsky mean by "the permanent revolution"?
3. What was the Workers' Opposition movement? What was its platform?
4. What brought about a breach between Stalin and Tito in 1948?
5. What are the four centers of international communism today?
6. In what ways are all Communist governments similar?

Questions to Think About

1. Why did Marx feel that capitalism must develop before communism could take over?
2. Why is there so little opposition to communism within the Soviet Union?
3. What is meant by the statement, "Power is an end in itself"?
4. Why has the Soviet Union permitted Yugoslavia to pursue an independent policy?
5. Why doesn't the Yugoslav brand of communism emphasize aggression and imperialism?

Books, Pamphlets, and Articles to Read

Paperback Books:

Brumberg, Abraham, ed., *Russia under Khrushchev.* Praeger, 1962; pp. 554-570.

Cronyn, George, *A Primer on Communism.* Dutton, 1961; Ch. 13.

Djilas, Milovan, *The New Class.* Praeger, 1957.

Roberts, Henry, *Russia and America.* Mentor, 1956; Ch. 10.

Seton-Watson, Hugh, *From Lenin to Khrushchev.* Praeger, 1960; Ch. 13.

Weyl, Nathaniel, *Red Star over Cuba.* Hillman Books, 1961.

Other Books

Laqueur, Walter and Labedz, Leopold, editors, *The Future of Communist Society.* Praeger, 1962; pp. 156-169.

Schapiro, Leonard, editor, *The U.S.S.R. and the Future.* Praeger, 1963; pp. 232-252.

Articles:

"The Mood Inside Russia's Satellites," Louis Fischer. *Saturday Review,* July 15, 1961.

"The U.S.S.R. and the Communist Bloc," Stephen Kertesz. *Current History,* Nov., 1961.

8

Life Under Communism in the Soviet Union

Before the Soviets sent their first Sputnik into space, many Americans tended to downgrade everything about Soviet technology and production. Now the pendulum has swung in the other direction.

Not long ago a *New York Times* correspondent in Moscow coined a word: "Sputnikitis." He defined Sputnikitis as an inferiority complex — common among Americans — which came from the notion that since the Soviets were first to launch space vehicles (October 4, 1957), and were ahead of the United States in putting a man into orbit, the Russians must be outdistancing us all the way down the line.

A sure cure for this illusion, the correspondent suggested, was a trip to Soviet Russia. There the visitor would notice that many of the articles and services we take for granted are simply not available, or are reserved for a favored few.

The Soviet achievements in space exploration and rockets have been made by ignoring the needs of the Soviet people. Many observers maintain that if the people were given the choice, they would gladly exchange rocket leadership for a better standard of living.

COMPARATIVE PURCHASING POWER, IN TIME WORKED

		IN U.S.A.	IN SOVIET RUSSIA
	SOAP Small cake	2.6 min.	28 min.
	SUGAR 1 lb.	3 min.	54 min.
	SHIRT Men's, cotton	76 min.	13 hr.
	DRESS Street, rayon	4 hr. 28 min.	65 hr.
	STOCKINGS Nylon	37 min.	7 hr.
	SUIT Men's, wool	23 hr.	244 hr.
	POTATOES 1 lb.	1.6 min.	6 min.
	SHOES Women's leather	5 hr. 13 min.	51 hr.
	EGGS 1 doz.	13 min.	2 hr. 8 min.
	BEEF rib roast, 1 lb.	12 min.	1 hr. 27 min.
	MILK 1 qt.	7 min.	36 min.
	BUTTER 1 lb.	19 min.	3 hr. 26 min.

This sentiment has been voiced in letters sent to Soviet publications. One letter, written by a Moscow factory worker, to the newspaper *Sovietskaya Rossia*, states:

It is time we stopped fooling ourselves about Sputniks and jet airplanes. Let's come down to earth — to ordinary shoes. I have one pair, which I've worn for four years. And why did they last that long? Because they were made abroad. I manage to do quite well with a trolley car, but I do want to live better and to have properly made clothes.

In many respects, living conditions in the Soviet Union have improved in recent years, although the quality of most products is still inferior to that of Western European products. But low quality is not the chief complaint. The chief complaint is the scarcity of many items in everyday use.

Occasionally, the Soviet shopper sees something he needs in a store window, only to discover that it is just for display and not for sale. Soviet publications have criticized the clothing industry for not producing sufficient quantities and varieties of cotton dresses, yet manufacturers are likely to have difficulty finding desired colors and fabrics.

Shortages are even more acute in rural areas than in the cities. Such essential items as mittens, overcoats, and *valenki* (thick, felt boots) are in short supply in various rural districts during the winter months. People often find it impossible to buy buttons, needles, nails, pens and pencils, writing paper, and other everyday essentials easily found in most countries.

The craving for consumer goods was demonstrated by thousands of Soviet citizens during the few weeks of the U.S. exhibition in Moscow in 1959. One of the Russian-speaking U.S. guides at the exhibition reported: "It was almost impossible for them [the Soviet people] to conceive of an American worker with enough money to buy some of the ordinary things we had on display."

There is no starvation in the Soviet Union. People now have enough to eat, with plenty of bread, potatoes, cabbage, cereals, and a fairly steady, though expensive, supply of meat and fish. Vegetables, fruit, butter, and eggs, though, are plentiful only at certain times of the year.

Right: Moscow's Red Square. Soviet guides make sure that tourists are shown only what the Kremlin wants them to see.

The Party leaders, however, do not suffer from shortages, because they have special stores for their exclusive use — stores well supplied with luxury and imported items, such as Czechoslovakian shoes and Chinese silk.

Guns versus Butter

Although production of consumer goods is gradually increasing, the emphasis remains on heavy industry, including armaments and various kinds of machinery. But there are also other factors to be taken into account if one wishes to understand why acute shortages persist.

First, in Russia before the Revolution there was a good deal of peasant and artisan hand production of clothes, shoes, and household utensils. This is not the case today.

Second, there has been a big movement of population from the country districts into the towns and cities. Out of a population of about 225,000,000 in the Soviet Union today, over 50 per cent are town dwellers — as compared with about 20 per cent in prerevolutionary Russia. City people are more dependent on factory production than the old-fashioned peasants, who often lived on a fairly self-sufficient basis, making what they needed at home.

Third, the quality of Soviet production in consumer goods is so poor that frequent replacement of worn-out and broken goods is necessary.

Among the inconveniences endured by Soviet housewives are the long lines they must wait in to make their purchases, sometimes three or four times a day. The Soviet newspaper *Pravda* reports that in some areas "it has reached the point where there are even queues for one's daily bread."

People in Soviet Russia usually have some money to buy things, although prices are deliberately kept high by the government. Nearly every city has a "free market," at which secondhand clothes, household utensils, nylon stockings, and other items can be bought without waiting in line, at prices

Muscovites wait in line to buy buttons, pins, brooches, and trinkets. The sign on the side of the store reads "Notions."

higher than in the government stores. In addition, there are black markets, operated furtively from suitcases, through which religious articles, American jazz records, and even foreign currencies change hands, despite the vigilance of the police.

Since 1953 there has been a fairly steady and noticeable increase in the supply of clothing, shoes, utensils, radios, television sets, and refrigerators, but this has only whetted the appetite of a people long deprived of comforts and luxuries. The Soviet government now finds itself assailed by a new problem: the larger the supply of goods, the greater the pressure for more. Addressing a group in Siberia in 1961, Khrushchev himself indicated an awareness of this when he said:

A man has one overcoat. Then when he begins to live better, he wants to have one overcoat for everyday wear and one for Sunday best. That is only natural, Comrades. But where are we going to get them?

Housing Problems

In the Soviet Union, the vast majority of families do not own their homes. They pay rent to the state, and the rents are low. The average Soviet citizen spends three to five per cent of his wages or salary for rent. High rents are not the problem. Poor quality is, and so is the scarcity of adequate housing.

The housing shortage was considered the number one problem by Soviet citizens responding to a questionnaire distributed by the youth newspaper *Komsomolskaya Pravda* and published in its October 7, 1960, issue. The shortage has plagued most Soviet citizens for many years. Official estimates show that since 1955 buildings have been going up at a fast rate in the larger cities. The Soviets are now turning out around 2,000,000 new dwelling units per year, but even at this rate it will be many years before there will be enough housing for the people in the cities.

The aim of Soviet planning is to have an apartment for each family. Today, many families are doubled up in the same apartment. An average new apartment consists of two rooms with its own kitchen and bathroom. The older housing typically consists of one room to a family of five, with 20 or 30 people sharing a single toilet and kitchen.

In the cities, new apartment buildings are being put up so fast that the construction is often faulty. Doors and windows are warped, and fixtures are of poor quality. There has been so much flaking of mortar from the sides of new buildings that the officials have ordered a wire net spread around many of the buildings to protect passers-by from falling mortar.

Until recently the law allowed a Soviet citizen to build and own his house, if it had five rooms or less. But in August,

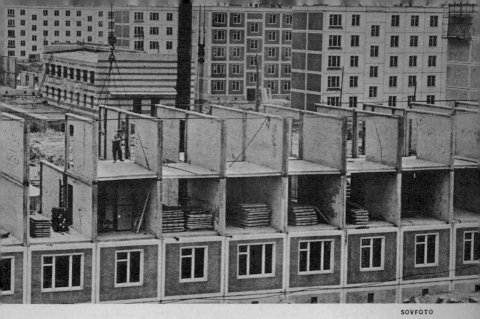

The housing problem constantly plagues city dwellers. This prefabricated building consists of 60 two-room apartments.

1962, the government announced that all single-family homes in towns and cities would be gradually abolished. Instead of individual homes, cooperative apartment houses are being erected, financed partly by the tenants.

In practice, though, even before the government decree, only a small number of privileged people (Party leaders, writers, artists, and others) could afford the luxury of a private house in a city. And even then, materials, labor, and land were often difficult to come by. Today a substantial number of well-paid people still have country homes, or *dachas*, where they live in the summer or on weekends, and which as yet have not been affected by the decree.

For most Soviet families the biggest single desire is for an apartment — in many cases, just one room — that they can have for themselves. They seek family privacy. The new Party program, adopted in October, 1961, promised that every city family would be "adequately housed" in a two-

room apartment by 1970. To do so would require a very large transfer of materials and manpower from building factories and armaments to building new houses at a rate far greater than the present one.

In rural areas, housing is primitive by Western standards. Most peasants live in log or clapboard huts called *izbas*, which have no plumbing and are heated by large stoves that burn charcoal. The peasants are grouped together in either *kolkhozes* (collective farms) or *sovkhozes* (state farms).

The principal difference between a kolkhoz and a sovkhoz is in ownership. All of the property on a kolkhoz, including the land, belongs to the kolkhoz. Each peasant family is allowed a small plot of land for its personal use, and sometimes a few livestock. The sovkhoz is strictly a state enterprise whose property — including livestock, produce, and implements — belongs to the state. Actually, however, because the government can convert collective farms to state farms at any time, the distinction is almost meaningless. Almost half the Soviet population now lives on collective farms, and accounts for more than 80 per cent of Soviet agricultural production.

Collective farms, such as this one in the Ukraine, are actually farm villages, averaging from 25 to 30 square miles each. There are about 44,000 of them in the Soviet Union.

Transportation

Many Soviet citizens will probably never have a chance to fly in a Soviet jet airliner. But most Muscovites at least will have an opportunity to ride on a much less expensive and equally famous mode of transportation — the Moscow subway. The Soviet government takes great pride in the attractively decorated Moscow subway with its mural paintings and mosaics. In other cities, transportation by bus and trolley is available and inexpensive. For most Soviet people, a car is out of the question — an unobtainable luxury.

Utopia Postponed

Since the policy of the Soviet government is to give priority to the production of machines and weapons rather than to better food and clothing, the leaders resort to promises of a brighter future. Perhaps the most spectacular in a long series of promises was the one made by Khrushchev in October 1961, when he announced the Party program for the next 20 years. This was a promise to catch up with and surpass the United States in the production of some consumer goods, such as food and clothing.

SOVFOTO

Little motor traffic plies Norilsk streets during the snow-filled Siberian winter. The scene is along the main street in March, 1962.

But two years later the Soviets suffered a serious setback in their economy. The disastrous grain harvest in 1963 forced them to purchase a billion dollars' worth of wheat abroad (including the U.S.). In December the Central Committee of the Party approved plans for greatly enlarging the chemical industry to provide fertilizers for farms. This will necessitate cutting expenditures in other areas, such as housing.

Despite Khrushchev's repeated promises of a better life in the future, the Soviet citizen can expect little immediate improvement in his everyday life. The Communist Party will still decide what goods he can buy and at what price. Shorter working hours still remain a dream. Soviet leaders are continuing to funnel so much money and manpower into heavy industry and armament that they are unable to meet consumer needs.

CHAPTER 8 — STUDY AIDS

Words and Names to Understand

"Sputnikitis"   free market   *sovkhoz*
consumer goods   *kolkhoz*   utopia

Checkup Questions

1. What factors account for the shortages in Russia? Where are the shortages most acute?
2. What is a "free market"? How does it differ from a "black market"?
3. Why are prices deliberately kept high by the Soviet government?

Questions to Think About

1. Why does the Soviet government emphasize the group, rather than the individual, in its sports programs and other activities?
2. How do you account for the low quality of housing and consumer goods in the Soviet Union?
3. How realistic is Khrushchev's promise that Russia will surpass the United States in material comforts by 1980?

Books, Pamphlets, and Articles to Read

Paperback Books:

Brumberg, Abraham, ed., *Russia under Khrushchev*. Praeger, 1962; pp. 153-321.

Cronyn, George W., *A Primer on Communism*. Dutton, 1961; Chs. 3, 4, 5, 10, and 11.

Schwartz, Harry, ed., *The Many Faces of Communism*. Berkley, 1962; Chs. 6, 7, 11, and 13.

The Soviet Union. Scholastic Book Services, 1962; Ch. 6.

Other Books:

Fitzsimmons, Thomas, *et al.*, *USSR*. HRAF, 1960; Chs. 3, 4, 10, and 16.

Gunther, John, *Inside Russia Today*. Harper, 1962; pp. 157-167; and Chs. 9 and 17.

Hindus, Maurice, *House Without a Roof*. Doubleday, 1961.

Articles:

"Khrushchev's Russia." *Atlas*, Oct., 1961.

"The Public Mood," Richard Pipes. *Harper's*, May, 1961.

"Russia's Social Elite," Mitchell Wilson. *Nation*, Aug. 26, 1961.

"Soviet Myths and Realities," Philip E. Mosely. *Foreign Affairs*, Apr., 1961.

"What Things Are Like Inside Russia," F. B. Stevens. *U.S. News*, Aug. 14, 1961.

9 *Education, Cultural Life, and Religion in the U.S.S.R.*

Since the beginning of Communist rule in Russia in 1917, Soviet leaders have recognized the importance of indoctrinating the young in Communist ideology. The Communist regime has always regarded the education of the youth as the cornerstone in establishing a firm foundation of a powerful Communist state.

Rewriting the Textbooks

One of the first tasks of the Communist regime was to arrange for the rewriting of textbooks to present the Bolshevik (Communist) orientation, not only to the history books, but to geography, languages, and other textbooks. This policy has been continued to the present day.

The Khrushchev regime is faced with the problem of rewriting textbooks to give the current interpretation of Stalin's place in Soviet history. It was much easier to remove Stalin's body from its place of honor beside Lenin's in the Kremlin tomb than it will be to remove the tributes to him from textbooks. Actually, the revision of textbooks was begun in 1956, after Khrushchev's secret speech before the 20th Congress of the Soviet Communist Party. The new *History of the Communist Party of the Soviet Union*, issued in 1959, makes few references to Stalin, but a revision had to be published in 1962 to include denunciations of his tyrannical rule.

Soviet Educational Philosophy

Strict control of what may be printed in textbooks is just one means of molding the minds of the young. Schoolteachers are under constant surveillance from local Party leaders, inspectors of the ministry, and the teacher's union, to make sure that official Communist doctrine is followed in the classroom. Since all schools are under centralized control, it requires only the deliberation of a few top officials to decide what may and may not be taught, and what may or may not be printed in textbooks and taught in classrooms.

Since the 1917 Bolshevik Revolution, Soviet education has undergone several changes. Immediately following the Revolution, there was an attitude of wide permissiveness. Students were encouraged to organize their own councils to participate in the management of the schools. No examinations were given. This policy was changed shortly after Stalin came to power. Rigid discipline was instituted, and the authority of the teacher was made supreme. Under Khrushchev there has been another change — a shift in emphasis from the study of the humanities to practical studies. At secondary-school level in particular, much time formerly spent on Russian literature, history, and social studies is now being devoted to "polytechnical" courses leading directly to jobs.

Denial of the dignity and freedom of the individual is part and parcel of Soviet education. All teaching is directed to ensure that the individual will serve the state, not as a free human being, but as an obedient subject of the regime. Stu-

A school in Moscow: After the required eight years in elementary school, qualified students go on to secondary school.

dents do not have the opportunities to develop to their full potential, in the direction their interests and abilities lead. Soviet education has a special purpose — to train the young to fill the quotas in industry, science, and services determined by the Soviet government. Nevertheless, the desire for an education is real among all the people. Parents imbue their children with the importance of education, and push them to get as much as they can under the restrictions that prevail.

The School System

Indoctrination in communism begins for many children as soon as they are able to talk. Because in most families both parents work, day nurseries have been set up at factories, government offices, and other places employing many workers. In these day nurseries loyalty to the leaders is taught in the kinds of games the children play.

Children enter elementary school at the age of seven and are required to attend for eight years. Pupils who do not qualify for further formal education after the eighth year are put to work or assigned to trade schools, where specialized courses prepare them for skilled work in factories, farms, and offices. Some go to school part time and work part time.

Because of the serious Soviet shortage of young workers (as a result of the loss of men in World War II, and the subsequent decline in the birth rate), only students of outstanding ability may continue for three more years in the secondary school. Here, in addition to gaining a general education, they are trained on the job in industry and receive a certificate when they graduate, enumerating the labor skills they have acquired.

In many parts of the U.S.S.R. the full school course for elementary and secondary school is still ten years. A law passed in 1958 provided for a gradual change-over to an eleven-year program. About one fourth of the students who enter the elementary school complete the secondary school program. Of those who do, about 12 per cent are admitted to the universities and professional or military institutes.

Until 1956, students at all levels, including the nursery schools, paid tuition fees. Today no tuition fees are charged, even in the universities. Parents still have to pay about 25 per cent of the cost for maintaining a child in nursery school, however.

At university level, the student receives a set sum of money for living expenses, which does not allow for any "treats." For students whose marks are "good" or "excellent," though, additional payments are made to keep incentive high.

Although university admission is on the basis of merit, there are other requirements. The applicant must have the approval of the Communist Party's youth organization, *Komsomol*, to certify his loyalty to the regime. Also, he must first complete one or two years of "productive labor." Exceptions may be made for students with outstanding talents, for training in critically undermanned professions.

Scientific and technological education is emphasized to prepare an increasing number of students for high-paying jobs in science, engineering, and the teaching of these subjects.

Communism in the Curriculum

At all levels of schooling, Soviet students are exposed to Communist doctrine. In the first three grades, indoctrination consists chiefly of comparing the "advantages" of the Communist system with the "backwardness" of prerevolutionary Russia. The picture of pre-Communist Russia, as presented in the schools, is the Russia of the 1880's and not that of 1914, by which time Russia had made noteworthy gains in public education and industrial development.

In the fourth grade, indoctrination includes study of "Conditions of Workers in Capitalist Countries" and "The Struggle of the World Masses against the Imperialist Warmongers." In both courses the United States is pictured as the chief villain among capitalist nations, ruled by a small clique that oppresses the working classes and provokes war for the enrichment of the capitalist class. The United States is described as a land of high unemployment, low income for working people, hopeless poverty, and poor medical care for all but the wealthy.

Throughout his schooling, the Soviet child is given a false picture of life in the United States. The accomplishments of the American democracy are either ignored or misrepresented. Soviet students learn nothing of the power of the people in a democracy to change their government officials. Racial discrimination in the United States is wildly exaggerated, and no reference is made to the progress that is being made in overcoming it. The high U.S. standard of living is described as nothing but a mirage for the vast majority of Americans.

The Soviet people are curious about life in America, but when told the truth many refuse to believe it. They cannot imagine that so many people can have so high a standard of living. After all, their own government has told them something quite different about life in America.

Youth Organizations

Away from school, Soviet young people are subjected to more forms of indoctrination. Much of this is done through government-sponsored youth organizations: the *Octobrists,* for children from five to eight; the *Pioneers,* for children from nine to fifteen; and the *Komsomol* (or Young Communist League), for those from 16 to 27.

Komsomol members applaud opening speaker at 14th Komsomol Congress, held in Moscow's Kremlin Palace in 1962.

SOVFOTO

These youth organizations, like their counterparts in other countries, engage in sports, hiking, amateur theatricals, chess, and other social activities. But that is not their main purpose. Their main purpose is to teach and train young people to obey the orders of the regime and to follow the principles of Communist doctrine. Their program also includes study of Communist Party theory and its application to everyday Soviet life. Members are trained to accept a strict discipline that requires them to report any disloyalty to the regime, even if it involves their own parents. No competing groups are permitted; the only way young people can participate is to join Communist-led organizations.

The Octobrists and the Pioneers include more than 90 per cent of the children in their respective age groups. The Komsomol is more selective. It often expels members for critical comments about the regime, for going to church, or for too much enthusiasm about Western ideas or clothes. Members of the Komsomol who have a record of loyal and zealous devotion to the cause may ultimately be rewarded by being admitted to the adult Communist Party. A good Komsomol record has other advantages, such as admission to the university, award of a scholarship, free vacations, or appointment to government jobs.

In the secondary (high) schools and universities, the Komsomol branch is expected to report to the authorities any political heresy on the part of faculty members. This has led to dismissal of instructors suspected of a lukewarm attitude toward any of the dogmas of the Party, and the ruination of their careers. (Another organization vigilantly on the lookout for heresy on the part of faculty members is the Communist Party committee, active in all universities.)

Physical Fitness

The Soviet government lays great stress on its physical-fitness program. The Union of Sports Societies and Organiza-

Massed Soviet soldiers form a platform on which gymnasts build a pyramid. Kremlin leaders consistently stress "collective" effort in all undertakings, including even sports.

tions of the U.S.S.R. and the Communist Party encourage participation in active sports through a program directed by the trade unions and the Komsomol. Their goal has been to raise the number of participants from 20,000,000 in 1959 to 50,000,000 in 1965. There are 200,000 sports clubs in existence in factories, schools, offices, state farms, collectives, and military, trade-union and police organizations. Workers take part in group exercises at their plants in the program of on-the-job calisthenics, which are encouraged by official publications as "a means of improving health and raising labor productivity."

Thousands of Soviet athletes participate in the annual sports parades on Physical Culture Day. These spectacles feature gymnasts engaging in vigorous exercises and stunts, impressive floats, and gigantic banners proclaiming the ideals of peace and Party loyalty.

In recent years the Soviet Union has won numerous honors abroad for the prowess of its athletes in the Olympic games and other international contests.

In sports, as in most other activities in the Soviet Union, the state stresses the group as the unit of society. This minimizes personal characteristics and tends to submerge the individual in the Communist collective. It also gives Party officials a means for keeping him in line. Through group activity, the individual can be indoctrinated with Party ideas and observed by the Party regulars.

Back in 1925 a resolution of the Central Committee of the Communist Party stated:

> Physical culture must be considered . . . as a means of rallying the broad masses of workers and peasants to the various Party, soviet, and trade union organizations through which the working and peasant masses are drawn into social and political life.

Control of Cultural Life

What Soviet citizens may read, what they may see at the cinema, at the theater, and on TV, and what they may hear on the radio, are all carefully selected to further the purpose of the Communist regime. Though there is strict censorship, the censor's task is actually very simple. No playwright, TV script writer or newspaper reporter would be

Yevgeny Yevtushenko has been criticized by Party conservatives for his poems, one of which protested Soviet anti-Semitism. He has said, however, that he would continue to speak out against abuses in Soviet society, in spite of any attempts to quiet him.

SOVFOTO

SOVFOTO

Alexander Tvardovsky, an editor of a leading Soviet literary magazine, has aroused controversy by advising young writers to tell "the full truth about life," and not merely follow the Party line. He and Yevtushenko, among others, are enjoying a partial relaxation of government controls over poets and writers—for the time being.

likely to submit any writing that remotely suggested doubt as to the supremacy of the Communist system.

The late Boris Pasternak, whose novel *Doctor Zhivago* gave a realistic and critical account of the Bolshevik revolution, was persecuted when his book was published in Italy. Moreover, he was not permitted to go to Sweden to accept the Nobel Prize for Literature.

Dimitri Shostakovich and other leading Russian com-

113

posers were forced to make public apologies for "deviating from Socialist realism," in their music. During Stalin's time some of Shostakovich's music was banned from public performance.

Soviet encouragement of originality and experimentation seems to be confined to science. Modern art is frowned on by Soviet authorities. The Soviet exhibition in New York City a few years ago, highlighted by a glittering reproduction of the first Sputnik, was notable for its dull art display — a roomful of Victorian-style landscapes and patriotic, poster-like portraits.

There has been one notable exception to the policy of keeping the Soviet people from reading views contrary to official Communist doctrine. In November, 1961, the Soviet newspaper *Izvestia* carried an interview conducted by its editor, Aleksei Adzhubei, Khrushchev's son-in-law, with President Kennedy in the United States.

A certain amount of what the Soviets call *samo-kritika*

"And so, my friends, you have seen dresses you cannot order, made out of fabrics you cannot buy."

KROKODIL

(self-criticism) is tolerated. For example, the Soviet humor magazine *Krokodil* publishes cartoons lampooning bureaucracy, red tape, and inefficiency. It makes jokes about the long lines at the stores, the shabby merchandise, and the favoritism practiced by minor officials. The target of the criticism, however, is never the Communist system or the top Party leaders. They become a safe subject for criticism only after they have been attacked by Khrushchev or some other top official.

Do the Soviet people enjoy the controlled cultural fare offered them under the censorship of a government authority? Foreign observers of Soviet life report that the Soviet people tend to ignore the subtle political propaganda and enjoy public performances for their artistry. In the areas of fiction, drama, stage, TV, and motion pictures there are signs of public boredom with the relentless barrage of Party propaganda. At the Moscow Art Theater, the most popular plays are those from the old Russian classics, written before the Communist Revolution, or Western plays (usually selected to picture the seamy side of capitalism). Although imported motion pictures are popular, the ones from the free nations are few and far between. The United States and the U.S.S.R. have an agreement to exchange ten motion pictures a year.

There is also a limited exchange of "live" artists — dancers, instrumentalists, orchestras, and singers. Under Stalin, American jazz artists could not have appeared in the Soviet Union. Under Khrushchev, the door has been opened to a few — Louis "Satchmo" Armstrong, the trumpeter; and Benny Goodman, clarinetist and orchestra leader. Goodman took a 19-piece orchestra and a female vocalist to the Soviet Union in the summer of 1962.

Religion Survives against Heavy Odds

Communism preaches atheism, denies the existence of God, and declares that "religion is the opium of the people."

115

Communists, in all countries, oppose religion because they do not recognize any authority beyond the state.

There were, and still are, many people in the Soviet Union who hold to religious beliefs their families have held for generations. Though the youth of the Soviet Union, since 1917, have been taught in school to cut themselves off from religion, their parents — unless they are Communists — usually hold firm to their faith in God, even though the opportunity to worship publicly may have been denied them because of closed churches.

For all its efforts to discourage religious belief, the Soviet government has not been able to extinguish it, and has not as yet dared take the extreme measure of closing all churches and eliminating the clergy.

In February, 1918, just a few months after the Bolsheviks seized power in Russia, orders were issued to start closing the churches. By 1930, of the 54,000 churches in operation before the Revolution, only about 5,000 were permitted to remain open. The government nationalized church property, restricted the clergy to the holding of services, and otherwise persecuted — even executed — many of them. At the same time it continued its propaganda campaigns against religion through the press, the radio, outdoor posters, in schools, and in theaters.

Organized groups of young people were released from school from time to time to participate in demonstrations against churchgoers. Many of the closed churches were converted into museums where religious statues and relics were displayed as objects of curiosity. Teachers suspected of holding to their religious beliefs were closely watched for signs of violating orders against any favorable references to religion.

Over the years, the Soviet government's campaign against religion has varied in intensity, to suit the immediate objectives of the regime.

When the Soviet Union became involved in World War II, Soviet authorities relaxed their antireligious activities. There was a reopening of many churches and seminaries, because the government wished to have all possible support for its war effort. After the war, however, antireligious campaigns were renewed.

The Russian Orthodox Church

Most of the Soviet people who hold to a religious faith belong to the Russian Orthodox Church, a powerful force in Russian life for centuries and one of the major Christian organizations of the world. The tsarist governments subsidized the Russian Orthodox Church, and the Russian Orthodox religion became the official faith. Of course it is no longer "official" since the Communist Party (and thus the Soviet government) has made all too plain its opposition to religion. Today the Orthodox Church and other church groups are merely tolerated by the government. To continue to be "tolerated," Orthodox Church officials and clergy cannot oppose government policy, are under the same restraints concerning freedom of speech as anyone else, and in many instances actively engage in Soviet propaganda against the United States. It can be said that the Orthodox Church officials and the Soviet government officials have an "understanding" which permits the church to exist as long as it does not interfere with government policy and decisions.

The head of the Orthodox Church is the Patriarch, who is responsible to the government body called the Council on Affairs of the Russian Orthodox Church. This group, appointed by the government, keeps an eye on all religious activity in the country. The Synod, a group of high ranking Orthodox Church officials, has traditionally worked out church problems and policies with the Patriarch. It still exists in the Soviet Union, but all of its decisions are kept in line with policies dictated by the Council.

According to figures supplied by the Russian Orthodox Church to the World Council of Churches, to which the Russian Orthodox Church was recently admitted, there are about 30,000 priests serving 20,000 Orthodox parishes in the Soviet Union today.

Other Religions

Other religious groups in the U.S.S.R. include the Old Believers (a branch of the Orthodox Church), Baptists, Roman Catholics, Jehovah's Witnesses, Lutherans, Jews, Moslems, and Buddhists — they are all targets of attack by the government.

The 500,000 Jews in Moscow have only three synagogues, and (according to the Soviet census of 1959) in all of the Soviet Union there are only 48 synagogues for a Jewish population of 2,268,000. Late in 1961, the only seminary in the country for the training of rabbis was closed.

The Baptists constitute a significant group in the Soviet Union, with about 512,000 adult members in some 5,000 congregations. More than a million Lutherans live in Latvia and Estonia, and some 1,235 Roman Catholic parishes exist throughout the U.S.S.R. There is some activity by Jehovah's Witnesses, a sect whose antimilitary point of view is unpopular with the Soviet government. Islam, the traditional religion of some 25,000,000 people in the Soviet Union, is also under severe pressure by the Soviet regime.

Church leaders jailed by Stalin have been released under Khrushchev, and religious training is now permitted in church schools. But appointments of high church officials must be approved by the government. In Poland, as well as in some of the other Soviet satellite nations, government antireligious campaigns do not succeed to the degree that they do in the Soviet Union. Ninety-five per cent of the Poles are said to attend church regularly. Most of them are Roman Catholic.

A Russian Orthodox priest blesses the traditional Easter cakes. With atheism a part of every child's education, churchgoers in the Soviet Union are officially frowned upon.

Anti-Semitism

There are many reports of a revival of anti-Semitism in the Soviet Union, with little or nothing being done by the regime to check it. The word "Jew" must be stamped on all internal passports carried by Soviet citizens of the Jewish faith, under a regulation requiring that a citizen's "nationality" be shown.

After the Revolution the Bolsheviks denounced anti-Semitism as being incompatible with the Communist ideals of brotherhood. However, in the 1930's the Stalin regime restricted the number of Jews who could hold prominent positions. When the state of Israel was established in 1948,

119

Soviet persecution of Jews was intensified, as Stalin reportedly suspected that those who lived in the Soviet Union were really loyal to the new state. The Yiddish theater was done away with, the publication of Yiddish books suspended, and their writers imprisoned or executed. Although the death of Stalin curbed the acts of terror, the present Soviet government still treats Jews as possible security risks and maintains the bans on Jewish cultural institutions.

The Fate of Buddhism

Buddhism, too, has suffered under the Communists. In mid-1960 a Soviet Buddhist delegation visited Cambodia, where it was received by both the Premier, Prince Sihanouk, and the Cambodian Minister of Religion. All of this gave the impression that Buddhism enjoys full freedom and an honorable status in the Soviet Union. However in a 1960 issue of the Soviet periodical *Nauka i Religiya (Science and Religion)*, the real situation was described. The journal gave a short survey of the fate of Buddhism in the three territories of the U.S.S.R. where it is the religion of the majority of the population. In Buryatia (in eastern Siberia), before the Revolution, there were 36 Buddhist monasteries with 16,000 *lamas* (Buddhist priests.) Now there are two monasteries and the number of lamas has dwindled to fewer than 100. In Tuva (Central Siberia) there are now about 100 lamas and no evidence of monasteries or temples remains, as compared with 22 temples and more than 4,000 lamas before the Revolution. In the Kalmyk Republic (North Caucasus), only one Buddhist temple remains.

Stepping Up the Attack

Attacks on all religions are again on the increase. The Soviet press and radio carried numerous reports of anti-religious activity in 1961. Among the acts carried out were the closing of 180 churches in the Volynsk Region of the

Ukraine "upon the demand of the workers," as well as mass closings of churches in the Chernigov Region. Reports from Moldavia indicate the closing of 25 churches and a number of Orthodox monasteries there, and the diversion of hundreds of monks and representatives of the clergy to "general, useful work." Of eight seminaries, three (in Kiev, Saratov, and Stavropol) were closed. Arrests of members of Orthodox, Pentecostal, and Jehovah's Witnesses sects were reported, with the sentencing of the former Archbishop of Chernigov to eight years' imprisonment for "speculation" and "expropriation" of parishioners' funds, and the sentencing of a group of Jehovah's Witnesses to seven years' imprisonment. An issue of *Komsomolskaya Pravda* called for administrative measures against parents who teach their children to believe in God. This persecution is not limited to the Orthodox Church, but affects representatives of other faiths as well.

In spite of the uprooting of many houses of worship in U.S.S.R., millions of persons still hold to their religious faiths. They worship in family groups at home, often at the risk of disciplinary measures by local Communist Party officials. The intensity of the present antireligious campaign is an indication of the regime's concern with the   ent increase in church attendance. Full propaganda force is being used to keep teen-agers out of church. But many young people have been attending anyway — some perhaps to find out for themselves just what a religious service is like.

For all of their efforts to discredit religion, the Soviet leaders have had to face up to a basic fact of human life: religious belief cannot be stopped by the issuance of orders. It can be discouraged by bringing up young people in ignorance of religion. And this is being done, even though the regime tolerates a limited number of open churches. But there is no doubt that this toleration is a temporary expedient, and that the ultimate goal is to eliminate religion as a force in the Communist society.

CHAPTER 9 — STUDY AIDS

Words and Names to Understand

ideology	*Pioneers*	Islam
Komsomol	atheism	Buddhism
Octobrists	Russian Orthodox Church	anti-Semitism

Checkup Questions

1. Describe the Soviet school system.
2. What is the main purpose of youth groups in the Soviet Union?
3. What types of criticism are permitted in the Soviet Union?
4. How has Soviet education changed since the Revolution?
5. What picture of the United States is given in Soviet schools?

Questions to Think About

1. Why is it necessary for the Communists to "rewrite" history?
2. What is meant by Karl Marx's phrase, "Religion is the opium of the people"?
3. How successful is the Communist antireligion program?
4. Why has there been a rise of anti-Semitism in the U.S.S.R.?

Books, Pamphlets, and Articles to Read

Paperback Books and Pamphlets:

Bereday, George, *The Changing Soviet School.* Houghton Mifflin, 1960.

Brumberg, Abraham, ed., *Russia under Khrushchev.* Praeger, 1962. "The Literary Scene"; pp. 341-440.

Cronyn, George W., *A Primer on Communism.* Dutton, 1961; Ch. 9.

Decter, Moshe, ed., *The Profile of Communism.* Collier, 1961; pp. 128-138.

Fedenko, Panas, *Khrushchev's New History of the Soviet Communist Party.* Institute for the Study of the U.S.S.R., Munich, 1963; Foreword (pp. vii-xi) and pp. 153-187.

Schwartz, Harry, ed., *The Many Faces of Communism.* Berkley, 1962; Chs. 8 and 9.

Other Books:

Colegrove, Kenneth, *Democracy Versus Communism* (2nd ed.). Van Nostrand, 1961; pp. 337-350.

Schapiro, Leonard, ed., *The U.S.S.R. and the Future.* Praeger, 1962; pp. 212-221.

Articles:

"Christ under Communism," Milton Mayer. *Harper's,* Aug., 1960.

"Our Image in the Soviet School Books," Nicholas DeWitt. *New York Times Magazine,* March 26, 1961.

"The Voice of a Dissenter," David Burg. *Harper's,* May, 1961.

The Communist Victory in China

Communism won an important victory when mainland China was overrun by the Chinese Communist armies in 1949. On September 21 of that year Mao Tse-tung, the Chinese Communist leader, proclaimed the establishment at Peking of the "People's Republic of China" and appointed Chou En-lai as Premier and Foreign Minister.

The Chinese Communist victory took place 32 years after the Bolshevik Revolution in Russia and was to some extent an outgrowth of the latter. The Chinese Communist leaders professed to follow the same masters: Marx, Lenin, and Stalin.

A Peasant Guerrilla Movement

Communism in China came into power by a path different from that of communism in Russia. Although the leaders in both China and Russia were Marxist intellectuals and professional revolutionaries, the revolutions took quite different forms. In Russia, it was the industrial working class that

123

Students at Peking's Petroleum Institute exercise to commands from a loudspeaker. Everyone— students, workers, even farmers — must perform exercises twice a day.

made up the rank and file of the Party, and it was the big cities where they worked — Moscow and Petrograd — that were first captured by the Communists. In China, communism was a peasant guerrilla movement and the Chinese Reds got control of wide areas of the countryside before they were able to capture the large cities. Working-class participation was slight. One reason for this was that China was basically an agricultural country. The number of factory workers was proportionately much smaller than it had been in Russia when the Communists seized power in 1917.

In the 1920's, Soviet agents flooded China. They had two objectives: (1) to set up a Chinese Communist Party; and (2) to get control of the rising Nationalist People's Party or *Kuomintang*. This party had been organized by the revolutionary leader Dr. Sun Yat-sen in 1912, following the overthrow of the Manchu dynasty, to further the cause of the new independent republic.

The Communist agents from the U.S.S.R. organized the Chinese Communist Party in Shanghai in 1921. One of the members of this original group was 31-year-old Mao Tsetung, the son of a wealthy farmer and a student of Marxism.

Mao was to become the leader of the Communist Revolution, and the small group of Party members was to grow to 17,000,000 by 1962.

For a time the chief Soviet agent, Michael Borodin, held considerable influence in the higher councils of the Kuomintang, and his aides helped that body with military and financial matters. An interesting but not widely known fact is that an obscure Brooklyn dentist, Dr. Maurice William, was instrumental in delaying the Communist take-over in China by 22 years. In 1924 Sun Yat-sen, after reading Dr. William's book, *The Social Interpretation of History*, completely repudiated his Marxist beliefs and devoted himself until his death to harmonizing the interests between the working classes and the capitalists. Sun Yat-sen died in 1925, and in 1927 his disciple and closest aide, Chiang Kai-shek, took over the Kuomintang. General Chiang purged the Communists, and from that time on the Kuomintang followed a consistent anti-Communist line.

Not only did the Kuomintang reject Soviet help, but the Chinese Communist movement itself seems to have maintained only slight contact with Moscow. Under the leadership of Mao Tse-tung, the Chinese Reds worked mostly among guerrilla bands in remote rural areas. Earlier the Chinese Communists had appealed to students and others along Soviet communism's lines, as a revolt against the wealthy classes of China and foreign "imperialists." (Much foreign capital — from Japan, Britain, and other countries — had been invested in Chinese industry, which was centered in Shanghai, Hankow, and Canton.)

In 1945, at the end of World War II, defeated Japanese troops withdrew from China. But that country was so exhausted by eight years of war, Japanese occupation, plundering, and governmental corruption that the task of restoring order proved beyond the power of Chiang Kai-shek. Currency inflation and the widespread lack of efficient local government helped to intensify Communist guerrilla activity. In addition, when the Soviet Union occupied Manchuria, it took over large quantities of arms which in turn were handed over to the Chinese Communists.

At this time the United States sent General George C. Marshall, former U.S. Secretary of State, to China to try and get the Chinese Nationalists and Communists to cooperate peacefully and govern China jointly. He did not succeed. Soon heavy fighting broke out between the Nationalists and the Communists. In this struggle the United States supplied weapons, ammunition, food, medicines, and other material to Chiang's Nationalists. And at first the Nationalist armies won important victories against the Communists.

Whether the United States should have done more to help the Nationalist government is still a matter of hot debate on which there may never be full agreement. With Japan made militarily helpless, a reasonably strong, friendly China was desirable to American security in the Far East. American public opinion, during the decisive years 1945-1949, was strongly influenced, directly and indirectly, in favor of the Chinese Communists. American sympathizers declared that

EASTFOTO

A column of women athletes, part of the annual May Day celebration in Peking, marches past Tien An Men Square.

the Communists were "agrarian reformers," and shouldn't be called Communists at all. The indirect influence took the form of stressing defects and weaknesses of the Nationalist government. The corruption and undemocratic tactics of the Chinese Nationalist Party, the Kuomintang, disappointed many U.S. citizens who, throughout World War II, had admired and respected Chiang Kai-shek. However, Americans who considered the Nationalist government unresponsive to the needs of the Chinese people did not face up to the fact that the fall of Chiang would mean a Communist take-over. They did not realize that in the long run this might be worse for China — and for the interests of the United States — than the Nationalist regime with all its faults.

In 1948 the tide of the Chinese civil war began turning in favor of the Communists. They gobbled up one region after another. The successes of the Communists were partly due to the discipline and the indoctrination of their soldiers. But perhaps even more important was the skillful Communist propaganda among the people of the villages and towns.

127

The Communists promised to take land away from rich land-owners and divide it up among peasants who had little or no land. The Communists said they would bring unity, order, and plenty to a China that had undergone years of fighting, disorder, and hunger.

By the end of 1949 the Communists had conquered all of mainland China. Chiang and 2,000,000 of his Nationalist followers fled to the island of Taiwan (Formosa), where the Nationalist government still has its headquarters.

To keep the Chinese Communists from invading Taiwan, a U.S. fleet stands guard in the strait between mainland China and Taiwan. The U.S. ships have orders to fight should the Communists launch an attack on Taiwan. The United States has also supplied the Nationalists with modern jet planes and other aid to strengthen their island fortress.

But the danger of a big shooting war always remains. Mao has threatened again and again that he plans to seize Taiwan by force and destroy the Nationalists. Mao's claims are supported by Khrushchev, whose note early in 1964 to all heads of governments calling for an end to war to settle territorial disputes described Taiwan as a different case. He called the island "an integral part of the Chinese state," and said, "Taiwan's unlawful occupation by American troops should be terminated."

Sino-Soviet Relations

Earlier evidence of friction between Moscow and Peking culminated in a major public dispute in mid-1963. The rivalry between the two countries for leadership of the international Communist movement resulted in waning Soviet influence among Asian Communist parties in particular, while what

In 1959 Khrushchev was the guest of Mao (left, clapping, and in big photo). Now there is friction between the two.

was once a unified and disciplined Communist bloc disintegrated. A number of somewhat more independent centers of political authority began to emerge.

For a time there was an impression among European Communists that Chinese communism was less rigid and ruthless than the Russian brand. For example, the Poles were inclined to attribute Khrushchev's decision not to use force against them in 1956 to Chinese intercession.

But these early speculations proved to be false. As it turned out, instead of taking a softer line than that of the Soviet Union, Red China has taken the position of extreme Communist conformity. Its leaders have launched violent attacks on Yugoslavia's Tito, berating him as an "opportunist" who has strayed from the true Communist path. On the question of war between the East and West, Red China takes a much tougher and more uncompromising line than the Soviet Union does. While Khrushchev has advocated "peaceful coexistence," leaders of Red China stress the fact that, in the world-wide Communist Revolution, war is practically inevitable — although they imply that the war would be started by the "imperialists."

There also have been differences in foreign policy. When the rugged little Balkan satellite, Albania, began to defy Khrushchev's leadership, and Soviet aid to Albania was stopped, China, despite its poverty, stepped in with funds and much-needed wheat. During the summer of 1960 the bulk of Soviet technicians were withdrawn from China – a serious loss.

However, the scars of Soviet-Chinese discord were covered up in a resolution that was adopted after long delay at a conference of 81 Communist parties in Moscow, toward the end of 1960. Each side made some concessions. On the Soviet Russian side of the ledger, Khrushchev obtained the signature of Red China's President Liu Shao-chi to his pet formula of coexistence. The Soviet Union's number one position among the Communist-ruled nations was acknowledged. Only the Soviet Union was given credit "for successfully carrying on the full-scale construction of a Communist society." On the other hand, Soviet Russia went along with

China in a statement to the effect that the change to communism might require violence. There were vehement denunciations of the United States, a declaration of all-out war against "colonialism," and condemnation of the Tito regime in Yugoslavia.

However, the Soviet-Chinese rift appeared again at the 22nd Congress of the Soviet Communist Party in October, 1961. This was marked by two events: Khrushchev's rebuke to the Albanian Communist Party, and his continued exposure of the crimes of Joseph Stalin. The Chinese Communists refused to endorse either of these attitudes.

The rift showed itself to be a yawning chasm when the Chinese Communists made public a letter addressed to their Soviet comrades on June 14, 1963, contradicting all major ideological policy guidelines set by Khrushchev. The letter wrecked a conciliation meeting in Moscow and led to violent mutual recriminations which continued until 1964, when some signs of abatement appeared.

In Anshan, Red China's "Pittsburgh," one state-owned iron and steel enterprise controls all—from mining to smelting.

EASTFOTO

In the Communist world, the Soviet Union is regarded as a "have" and China as a "have-not" country. The living standard in the Soviet Union, though vastly lower than that of the United States, Canada, or western Europe, is luxurious by comparison with that of the Chinese. Moreover, the Soviet Union seems to have made nearly all the territorial gains it can hope for, while China has not been able to occupy Taiwan or lands on its border.

It would be a mistake to attach great hopes to the rift between the two totalitarian giants. What unites them is still stronger than what divides them. The Chinese are too far behind the Russians in military and economic strength to risk an all-out break. Indeed, there is danger that Chinese pressure may force Khrushchev to behave in a more warlike manner than he might on his own initiative.

Communist China's Imperialism

Communist China has been at least as aggressive as the Soviet Union with respect to the seizure of foreign territory and the extermination of independent nations. North Korea was the first to fall to the Red Chinese (see Chapter 5). Only U.N. intervention in South Korea forced the invaders to retreat north of the 38th parallel.

Another Chinese imperialist act was the seizure of Tibet in 1951. When the Tibetan people revolted in 1959, the Red Chinese ruthlessly killed an estimated 90,000 Tibetans and forced the Dalai Lama, Tibet's religious and political leader, to flee. Also in 1959 Chinese troops occupied some 12,000 square miles of India's northwestern territory and claimed 51,000 square miles farther east. In October, 1962, they again invaded a peaceful India, which asked and received U. S. military aid. Two months later the Chinese Reds had ordered a cease-fire and offered to negotiate a settlement. The Indians agreed to negotiate, provided the Chinese first move out of the territory they had seized in 1959. By early 1964 the dispute had still not been settled.

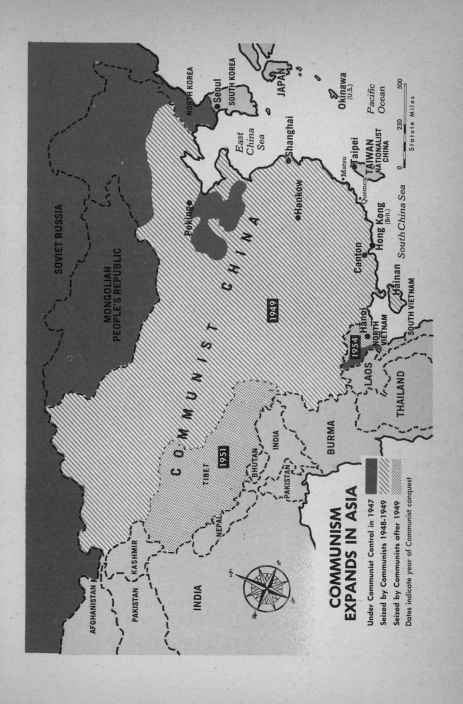

COMMUNISM EXPANDS IN ASIA

Under Communist Control in 1947

Seized by Communists 1948–1949

Seized by Communists after 1949

Dates indicate year of Communist conquest

SOVIET RUSSIA

MONGOLIAN PEOPLE'S REPUBLIC

C O M M U N I S T   C H I N A

1949

Peking

Hankow

Shanghai

East China Sea

NORTH KOREA

Seoul

SOUTH KOREA

JAPAN

Okinawa (U.S.)

Pacific Ocean

Matsu

Taipei

TAIWAN NATIONALIST CHINA

Quemoy

Hong Kong (Brit.)

Canton

Hainan

South China Sea

TIBET

1951

NEPAL

BHUTAN

INDIA

BURMA

THAILAND

LAOS

NORTH VIETNAM

Hanoi

1954

SOUTH VIETNAM

INDIA

KASHMIR

PAKISTAN

AFGHANISTAN

PAKISTAN

0   250   500

Statute Miles

The long shadow of Communist China's power has fallen over Southeast Asia as well. Chinese military aid helped Communist rebels take over part of the colony of French Indochina during the early 1950's. In 1954 French Indochina was partitioned into four countries: Communist North Vietnam, pro-Western South Vietnam, and neutral Laos and Cambodia. Recently the Chinese Reds have been aiding Communist rebels in Laos in their efforts to overthrow the country's government. Chinese aid has taken the form of money, weapons, and in some cases troops.

Communist China also stepped up its military and economic assistance to its satellite, North Vietnam. This, in turn, enabled the North Vietnamese Communists to carry on a guerrilla war against the government of neighboring South Vietnam. Red guerrillas infiltrating from the North gradually gained control of large areas of South Vietnam's countryside. Following the violent overthrow and death of President Diem and his powerful brother in an internal coup late in 1963, the United States renewed its commitment to defend the freedom of South Vietnam.

Troubles at Home

Even as they pursue their ambitious plans for conquest abroad, the Chinese Communist leaders have been faced with mounting problems on the home front. Some of these problems stem from the "Great Leap Forward," a campaign of forced industrialization begun in 1958 with the aim of making Red China a leading industrial and military power. At that time, factory workers and peasants were forced to put in a 12- or 14-hour workday in order to increase production. Millions of peasants were herded into sprawling farms called "communes," where they lived in barracks, ate in mess halls, and marched to and from their work in the fields.

It soon became apparent, however, that the "Great Leap Forward" was a failure in spite of industrial gains. The lack of normal family life in the communes, the extreme regimentation, and an inadequate standard of living caused a serious drop in morale. At the same time the inefficiencies of the Communist system, the overemphasis on industry, and the lack of incentives for farmers produced a drastic decline in agricultural production. For three years after the "Great Leap Forward" Red China suffered staggering crop failures.

The resulting food shortages left millions of Chinese on the brink of starvation. As criticism of the government mounted, the iron-fisted rule of the Communists became more oppressive than ever. Opponents of the regime were subjected to "brainwashing," imprisonment, and frequently execution. Seeking freedom and an end to their hunger, tens of thousands of Chinese refugees flooded into the British colony of Hong Kong, off the southeast coast of Asia. In 1963 the food situation improved somewhat, largely because the communes were abolished and the peasants were permitted to cultivate their own individual plots. The agricultural organization in China today approaches the Soviet collective-farm pattern. Neither country has solved its farm problems. Both have purchased wheat from the "capitalist West."

Members of the Nanyuan People's Commune, just outside Peking, listen to the Central Committee's latest instructions.

CHAPTER 10 — STUDY AIDS

Words and Names to Understand

Kuomintang   "agrarian reformers"   communes

Manchu dynasty   Dalai Lama   brainwashing

Checkup Questions

1. In what ways did the Chinese and Russian revolutions differ?
2. How was American public opinion influenced in favor of the Chinese Communists during the years 1945-1949?
3. What concessions did the Red Chinese and Russians make at the 1960 Party conference to resolve their differences?
4. What foreign territory has Communist China seized in recent years? To what countries has it given military aid?
5. Why was Red China's "Great Leap Forward" a failure?

Questions to Think About

1. What were the primary reasons for the Communist victory over the Nationalists in 1949?
2. Why was a strong, friendly China important to American security in the Far East after World War II?
3. Why does Red China feel it so important to take over Taiwan?
4. Why has there been increasing friction between Red China and the Soviet Union in recent years?

Books, Pamphlets, and Articles to Read

Paperback Books:

Barnett, A. Doak, *Communist China and Asia.* Vintage, 1960.

Bell, Oliver, *The Two Chinas.* Scholastic Book Services, 1962.

Seton-Watson, Hugh, *From Lenin to Khrushchev.* Praeger, 1960; Ch. 14 and pp. 376-383.

Other Books:

Mehnert, Klaus, *Peking and Moscow.* Putnam, 1963; pp. 354-385.

Articles:

"Communist Solidarity and Sino-Soviet Rivalry," Harold Fisher. *Current History,* Sept., 1961.

"Education in Red China," William Benton. *Saturday Review,* July 15, 1961.

"Khrushchev and China," Edward Crankshaw. *The Atlantic,* May, 1961.

"The Sino-Soviet Conflict: Origins and Present Prospects," K. Pavlov. *Bulletin of the Institute for the Study of the U.S.S.R.,* Munich, November, 1963, pp. 3-19.

"Stalin and China," George F. Kennan. *The Atlantic,* May, 1961.

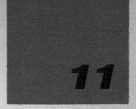

The Communist Pattern of Conquest

On the second day of March, 1919, a small group of men met in Moscow to plan a world revolution. They had been called by Lenin and Trotsky to organize the Comintern (Communist International) — a union of Communist parties throughout the world. There were only 35 voting delegates present. The majority were obscure revolutionaries who had been caught in Moscow and who had no authority to speak for political groups in their native countries. Nevertheless, they set down a blueprint of Communist expansion with world domination as its goal.

The following year, 217 delegates from 41 countries attended the Congress. They further outlined the plan of world conquest and adopted 21 rules for admission to the Comintern. These included direct authorization for mutiny and treason. For example:

> Persistent and systematic propaganda must be carried on in the army, where Communist groups should be formed in every military organization. . . . Each Party desirous of affil-

iating with the Comintern should be obliged to render every possible assistance to the Soviet Republics in their struggle against all counterrevolutionary forces.

In addition, all Communist parties were required "to create everywhere a parallel illegal apparatus, which at the decisive moment should be of assistance to the Party to do its duty to the Revolution."

The Grand Strategy

The Communist strategy, as the world now sees, uses many devices to gain its ends: force or threat of force, subversion, trade, propaganda. At the beginning, the main ambition of the Communist Party was to duplicate the Russian Revolution of 1917 in other countries. The Comintern set out to accomplish this.

It regarded as the most likely targets for Bolshevik-type revolutions the industrial countries of Western Europe and North America, because they were the most advanced industrially. But the Communists were ambitious; they also began to stir up trouble in the less advanced countries of Asia and the Middle East. Communist parties throughout the world were ordered to give aid to "revolutionary liberation movements in colonial lands," to help them throw off "imperialist" control.

The plan was clever. In Asia, where industry was almost nonexistent and the working class still weak, Communists were instructed to support non-Communist revolutionary movements while retaining their own organizations. The Indian Communist Party, for example, worked with the revolutionary National Congress. In China, too, the Chinese Communists rallied to support Sun Yat-sen's Kuomintang in 1924.

With World War II came holocaust and upheaval. Millions of people were torn loose from their old moorings. As Soviet Russia's Red Army pushed back Hitler's forces and advanced from the Volga to the Elbe, it brought with it Communist political and economic control, the one-party system, and the secret police.

Latvia, Lithuania, Estonia, and two fifths of Poland had been annexed by the Soviet Union before Hitler's attack. Now Communist controls, operated by both Soviet Communists and local Party members, were clamped down on the other occupied countries. Puppet regimes were set up in the reshaped Poland and in Romania, Hungry, Bulgaria, Czechoslovakia, and Eastern Germany. One-party rule, the secret police, Party monopoly over information and education, state ownership of industries, and the herding of peasants into collective farms were put into effect everywhere.

Thus, in the bloody aftermath of World War II, the Soviet leaders wielded their control over almost one hundred million people of east-central Europe. World War II made possible the expansion of communism in yet another continent — Asia. The greatest Communist victory since the Bolshevik Revolution of 1917 was the establishment of Communist rule in mainland China in 1949 (see Chapter 10).

The Methods of Communist Propaganda

Communist propaganda has an arsenal of weapons at its command. Some strike with the impact of a sledgehammer. Others stab with the cruel precision of a bayonet. Some are disguised and do not seem like weapons at all. A favorite method of the Communist propagandist is the "Big Lie" — based on the proposition that the masses will accept a monstrous falsehood more readily than a small one. Other propaganda techniques include appeals to group interests and prejudices, such as anti-imperialism, anti-Catholicism, anti-Semitism. Some of these appeals are subtle; some are blatant.

One method of psychological warfare used by the Soviets is a strategy of intermittent terror. They blow hot and cold: one day fierce threats, the next day soothing reassurances.

The effect of this treatment is a quick shift from fear to hope, which utterly confuses foreign public opinion. A good illustration of this method may be found in the following two contrasting statements made by Premier Khrushchev within a span of two months.

Here is Khrushchev the threatener, telling the Supreme Soviet (Parliament) on January 14, 1960:

> War would begin in the heart of the warring countries; moreover, there would not be a single capital, not a single major industrial or administrative center, not a single strategic area which would not be subjected to attack, not only during the first days, but during the first minutes of war.

And here is Khrushchev, the soothing peace lover, speaking to the Soviet-Indian Friendship Society, on March 4 of the same year:

> Analyzing the atmosphere which has arisen in the world in relations between peoples and governments, I am firmly convinced that all the conditions now exist for the preservation and strengthening of peace. Not only I myself, but all my friends who have made a realistic assessment of the international situation think so.

UP

Premier Khrushchev "registers his displeasure" during an address to the U.N. General Assembly by Prime Minister Macmillan of Great Britain. The incident took place four months after the collapse of the 1960 summit conference in Paris.

Khrushchev has used this technique repeatedly in dealing with the Western powers over Berlin. In his talk with President Kennedy in Vienna, in June, 1961, and on many other occasions, Khrushchev took the "hard" line: the Soviet Union would sign a treaty with its puppet regime, the so-called German Democratic Republic, in an attempt to force the Western Allies out of West Berlin. Then, during the autumn of 1961, Khrushchev changed tactics, calling off his December 31 deadline for the conclusion of the peace treaty. He hinted that the Soviet Union and the Western powers could negotiate an agreement on the status of West Berlin without dealing with the East Germans.

One of the trademarks of Soviet propaganda is a familiar principle of advertising: the use of repetition to produce a desired image. In the U.S.S.R. and its satellites the popular slogan — the catch phrase — assails the eyes of newspaper readers and blares from the radio and TV, telling the citizens to work, to play, to think, along government lines.

Both at home and abroad the Soviets have a special vocabulary. For example, America is always called "imperialist" and "colonialist," although it has neither empire nor colonies. And it is accused of "warmongering" if it tries to hold lines of defense against Soviet expansion. On the other hand, Communist activities are described in glowing terms. The nations under Soviet control are called "people's democracies" or "people's democratic republics." Communists are fond of using such phrases as "peaceful coexistence," and they grandly describe the Communist system as "the wave of the future." In fact, a whole list of words, such as "peace," "freedom," "elections," have been corrupted by Soviet misuse. "Socialism," which originally meant peaceful state control of production, has been distorted to mean rule through police terror. "Education" means teaching the young to parrot the Communist line, rather than to think for themselves. And in a "democracy" only one party appears on the ballot.

Shortly after his inauguration, President Kennedy met with Premier Khrushchev to clarify their respective points of view.

Subversion and Infiltration

In his recently published work *Kremlin Target: U.S.A.*, Donald C. Dunham states that "The Kremlin has fashioned out of propaganda the most powerful non-military weapon of national aggression the world has ever known."

One of the reasons Soviet espionage is so formidable and so difficult to detect is the ability of Soviet spy rings to recruit foreign agents. Every Communist citizen of a non-Communistic country is bound by Party discipline to work for the downfall of his own government. The many exposures of Soviet spy rings operating in the United States, Canada, Japan, and various European countries revealed that these operations were invariably helped by local Communists or persons who were emotionally attracted to communism.

The espionage organization established in Japan by Richard Sorge, a German Communist in the guise of a Nazi journalist, was composed of Japanese and Germans — not of Soviet Russians. The notorious Canadian spy ring which was exposed by Igor Gouzenko, a Soviet citizen employed as a code clerk by the Soviet Embassy in Ottawa, was made up of Canadian citizens, including members of the Canadian Communist movement. The Communists who betrayed nuclear-weapons secrets, people like Klaus Fuchs and Alan Nunn May in Great Britain and Julius and Ethel Rosenberg in the United States, were not Soviet citizens.

The problem of how to forestall treason of this type is a fairly new and difficult one. Fifty years ago it would have been a matter of no particular concern if a man with access to military, scientific, or industrial secrets was in sympathy with communism. There was then no Communist power to which he would have been tempted, or perhaps obligated, to betray his information. The creation of such a Communist power center in Moscow drastically changed this situation.

It is of the utmost importance for the U.S. government to keep Communist Party members and sympathizers from infiltrating government posts or other positions where they may threaten the safety of the nation. The question of how to deal with persons whose allegiance is directed to a foreign government is not a simple one for free societies. For the very steps that the government must take to prevent such individuals from occupying positions of authority may at the same time suppress their freedom of speech, right of privacy, and other basic rights which the United States, among other nations, guarantees through its constitution. A free society, if it is to remain free, must tolerate freedom of thought and expression. But it is under no obligation to commit suicide by permitting conspirators in the service of a foreign power to make free with its military, diplomatic, and scientific secrets.

The International Organization

When Marxists talk about socialism and communism, they often speak of the *First, Second,* and *Third Internationals.* These groups are important in Socialist and Communist history.

Cubans stage a propaganda assault on North American publications during a Havana carnival. Among the targets are *The New York Times* and Spanish editions of *Reader's Digest.*

The *First International,* originally named the International Workers' Association, was founded by Marx in 1864 in London. Through it he hoped to bring together the working people of all lands, to realize the aims of his *Communist Manifesto.* But its members could not agree. It was disbanded after a congress held at Philadelphia in 1874.

The *Second International,* sometimes called the Socialist International, was organized in Paris in 1889 and established its headquarters in Brussels. Most European Socialist parties joined it. Some of its members wanted to revise some features of Marxism. They believed that an orderly series of changes, by legal, democratic processes, could slowly improve social conditions. This International still exists, but it was badly weakened by its failure to prevent World War I.

The *Third International,* created in Moscow in 1919 by the Bolsheviks after their victory, is also known as the Communist International, or Comintern (see page 137). The Comintern met throughout the 1920's and 1930's to direct the strategy of the world revolution. This strategy changed from time to time, depending on world conditions and on the local conditions in the various nations.

In some countries, the Communist Party was ordered to organize new trade unions; in others it was told to join unions already in existence and try to convert their leadership to Communist ideas. The local Communist Party might be friendly with Socialist and labor parties one day and denounce them as "bourgeois" the next. During the 1930's Communist parties abroad joined other groups to oppose Hitler and Mussolini, but the Comintern reversed its position when Stalin signed the treaty of nonaggression with Hitler in 1939.

World War II presented serious obstacles to the direction of Communist parties from an international center. This, in addition to Stalin's desire to improve relations with the Western Allies, brought about the end of the Comintern on May 22, 1943.

After the war, the Communist parties of the Soviet Union and Eastern Europe, along with those of France and Italy, met in Poland and organized the *Cominform,* or Communist Information Bureau. The name was changed, but the purpose was the same, namely to promote communism throughout the world. The Cominform set up headquarters in Belgrade, Yugoslavia, and started on its first job: to consolidate strength among the satellite states along U.S.S.R. borders, and to keep Western influence out of Communist countries.

Shortly after its inception the Cominform took the following actions:

1. It set out to destroy Socialist and peasant parties in Eastern Europe.

2. It supported the Communist coup in Czechoslovakia which brought that country under Soviet domination in February, 1948.

3. It ordered Communist parties in France and Italy to organize strikes against the government.

U.S. Communist Party leaders Elizabeth Flynn (left) and Henry Winston (second from left) are greeted in Moscow by delegates to the 22nd Soviet Party Congress in 1961.

4. It carried on propaganda against U.S. activities in Europe, such as the Marshall Plan.

5. It expelled the Yugoslav Communist Party for defying Stalin's attempts to dominate Yugoslavia in June, 1948.

This last act backfired. Communists throughout the world disagreed over the expulsion of Tito, and many in countries outside of the Communist bloc resigned from the Party. The dissension lasted until the death of Stalin, in 1953. After Khrushchev's reconciliation with Tito, the U.S.S.R. announced on April 17, 1956, that the Cominform had been dissolved.

In its place, however, was the Warsaw Pact, a Soviet-inspired agreement signed in 1955. It established a joint military command over the Soviet Union, Poland, Bulgaria, Albania, Czechoslovakia, Romania, Hungary, and East Germany. By making East Germany a full member of the pact, the Soviets justified an arms build-up there, to offset West Germany's membership in NATO in 1954.

Communist Parties in Non-Communist Countries

Although organized opposition is not permitted in Communist-ruled countries, quite the reverse is true in non-Communist lands where Communist parties exist legally. These Communist parties loyal to Moscow faithfully follow every twist and turn of Soviet foreign policy.

One example is the behavior of the Communist Party in the United States. In the years before the United States entered World War II, and as long as Stalin denounced Hitler, the U.S. Communists proclaimed themselves to be ardent defenders of peace and democracy, and against war and fascism. But when Hitler and Stalin signed their secret treaty in August, 1939, and began to divide up Eastern Europe between them, the U.S. Communists, like Communists all over the world, forgot their attacks on Hitler and blamed Britain and France for starting World War II. The war became an "imperialist war," from which America must hold aloof, even if Hitler won.

The U.S. Communist Party turned another somersault the day after Hitler invaded the Soviet Union, in June, 1941. From that moment on American Communists declared the war was being fought for "democracy" and "justice," and they urged the United States to enter the war immediately. Just as the war came to an end, and the conflict of purpose between the United States and the U.S.S.R. became evident, the U.S. Communists took up the defense of each Soviet aggression, attacked U.S. policy as "imperialist," "reactionary," and "colonialist," and denounced the United States as exclusively responsible for the Cold War.

Individuals in the U.S. Communist Party who could not stomach these maneuvers had no choice but to quit the Party, which a great many did. Since 1928 the U.S. Party has remained in the hands of a group that is ready to follow any instructions from Moscow, even if it means repudiating the "line" established only a few weeks before.

Communist Party leaders in the United States are now contesting in the courts conviction for refusing to register the Party as an agency of a foreign power and for not supplying the names of its members, as required by the Internal Security Act of 1950. The Party's membership is estimated by the F.B.I. to be about 10,000. They try to gain control of some of the trade unions, civic groups, and other organizations, but rarely succeed in doing so. The AFL-CIO leadership is vigilant about keeping Communists out of office. A small group of Communist Party members or Soviet sympathizers, sometimes even a single person, may influence the policy of an organization or institution where the vast majority of members or employees are non-Communist Americans of unquestioned loyalty to their country.

In Western Europe only two Communist parties — the French and the Italian — display any real political strength. In France, the Communist vote has fluctuated from 25 to 28 per cent of the total, though the support of Communist candidates has declined under General de Gaulle's centralized control of French affairs since 1958. In Italy, the Communists usually poll a little more than one fifth of the vote in national elections; until 1962 they had a working alliance with a party of left-wing Socialists headed by Pietro Nenni, which brought the combined strength of the two groups to somewhat over one third of the vote cast. In April, 1963, elections, one out of four Italians voted Communist. Later that year, Nenni and the Socialist party agreed for the first time to participate directly in a center-left government, drawing away from their old Communist allies.

In the Western Hemisphere, communism now has a base of operations in Cuba. In other Latin American countries Communist influence has fed on social unrest, on extreme social contrasts (a few very rich, many very poor), and on a traditional fear and envy of the United States.

In Indonesia, the largest Communist Party (PKI) outside the Communist bloc claims 2,000,000 members, and has received President Sukarno's public endorsement as a legitimate participant in the nationalist movement.

Manipulation of Trade

In addition to the bristling, steel-fortified borders, the Soviet Union has a taut control of trade which can be a life-and-death threat to a satellite that gets out of line. The state monopoly on foreign trade makes it possible to shift orders from one country to another for political purposes in a series of rewards and punishments: now offering trade as bait, now cutting it off as a reprisal.

Similarly, the Soviets can use foreign trade to political advantage. They may, for example, dump certain commodities on the world market and sell them below prevailing prices in order to create an economic crisis. This can prove most effective against a country that depends primarily on the export of a single commodity.

Broken Treaties and Promises

The chief obstacle in the way of reaching a satisfactory and lasting settlement with the Soviet Union is the complete indifference of its rulers to their own pledged word. Here is a list of ten solemn treaties concluded by the Soviet government and broken at the first convenient opportunity:

Treaty or Pledge	*How and When Broken*
Recognition of the independence of Georgia, May 7, 1920	Georgia invaded and forcibly annexed to the Soviet Union February 11, 1921
Treaty of nonaggression and neutrality with Lithuania, September 28, 1926; Renewed May 6, 1931	Lithuania forcibly annexed August 6, 1940
Treaty of nonaggression with Finland, January, 1932	Soviet troops invade Finland November 30, 1939

149

Treaty or Pledge	How and When Broken
Treaty of nonaggression with Latvia, February 5, 1932	Latvia forcibly annexed August 5, 1940
Treaty of nonaggression and amicable settlement of disputes with Estonia, May 4, 1932	Estonia forcibly annexed August 3, 1940
Treaty of nonaggression with Poland, July 25, 1932	Poland invaded by Soviet forces and partitioned with Nazi Germany, September, 1939
Yalta agreement with United States and Great Britain, February, 1945, providing for free, unfettered elections in Poland, and democratic institutions in East European countries	Systematic and persistent violations of these promises leading to transformation of Poland and other countries occupied by the Red Army into one-party dictatorships
Treaty pledging support only to Nationalist government of China, August, 1945	Systematic violation of this treaty by giving aid to Chinese Communists
Agreements of 1945 and 1949 with the United States, Great Britain, and France, providing for freedom of movement between East and West Berlin	Erection by Soviet puppet government in East Germany of a wall, sealing off East Berlin from the rest of the city
Statement by Khrushchev that the Soviet Union would never be the first to resume nuclear testing	Soviet resumption of a series of powerful atmospheric blasts on August 30, 1961

It is this habitual bad faith by the Soviets that makes it difficult for the Free World to place any reliance upon a paper agreement with them.

CHAPTER 11 — STUDY AIDS

Words and Names to Understand

Comintern   treason   Cominform
psychological warfare   Warsaw Pact   Internal Security Act of 1950

Checkup Questions

1. How did World War II make possible the expansion of communism in Europe and Asia?
2. Why has Soviet espionage been so successful throughout the world?
3. How do Communist parties in non-Communist lands react to the constant changes in Soviet foreign policy? Give examples.
4. How do the Soviets use trade to control their satellites?

Questions to Think About

1. Why were the more industrially advanced nations better targets for Bolshevik-type revolution than the less advanced nations?
2. How effective have the "intermittent terror" and "Big Lie" techniques been as Cold War weapons for the Communists?
3. How can a free society meet the threat of Communist infiltration without suppressing basic freedoms?
4. How effective were the actions taken by the Cominform after its formation?

Books, Pamphlets, and Articles to Read

Paperback Books:

Decter, Moshe, ed., *The Profile of Communism*. Collier, 1961; Ch. 4.
Weingast, David E., *This Is Communism*. Oxford, 1961; Ch. 7.

Other Books:

Dunham, Donald C., *Kremlin Target: USA*. Ives Washburn, 1961.
Fitzsimmons, Thomas, *et al.*, *USSR*. HRAF, 1960; Chs. 13 and 14.
MacInnes, Helen, *Neither Five Nor Three*. Harcourt, Brace, 1951.
Philbrick, Herbert, *I Led Three Lives*. McGraw-Hill, 1952.

Articles:

"The Communist Party, USA," Harold C. Martin. *Saturday Evening Post,* May 19, 1962.
"Peaceful Competition along Russia's Border," Harrison Salisbury. *New York Times Magazine,* Apr. 8, 1962.
"Plus ça Change," Pierre Naville. *Atlas,* Apr., 1962.

12

Why Do Some People Become Communists?

It is easy to understand why a country submits to Communist rule where the Red Army has marched in and set up the Communist system, with its far-flung organization of secret police, and its threat of death or the concentration camp for objectors. But it is not so easy to understand why individuals become Communists of their own free will in countries that have the democratic system.

Why do some fairly well-to-do, educated people of middle-class origin betray political and scientific secrets to Communist agents in the United States or join Soviet spy rings in Canada? Or, to take a different case, why do some peasants in an Oriental country like South Vietnam help Communist guerrillas, even though they know — or should know — that hundreds of thousands of their fellow villagers have fled from intolerable conditions in the Communist-ruled northern part of their divided country?

Some of the Reasons

There is no simple answer. The problem is complex because the motivations of individuals toward communism vary considerably from country to country and from one period of history to another. The economic, social, and psychological conditions in North America and Western Europe are quite different from those in the economically retarded lands of Asia, Africa and South America.

Here are ten reasons why some individuals are attracted to communism:

1. Poverty, with no hope of improvement.
2. Racial or social discrimination.
3. Ignorance and illiteracy. (The inability to read or write makes an individual susceptible to Communist word-of-mouth propaganda.)
4. Loss of religious faith. (Some persons become attracted to communism because they have no deep understanding of their spiritual faith, or because they misunderstand the true nature of communism.)
5. Resentment toward social backwardness and real or alleged corruption in government.
6. Mistaking communism for a system that stands for "peace," the righting of wrongs, and giving the "underdog" his chance.
7. Yearning for short cuts to an ideal society; impatience with the gradual, orderly democratic process.
8. Having a too-rosy picture of life under communism in such "utopias" as the U.S.S.R. and China. (Such misconceptions are fostered by Communist propaganda publications in non-Communist countries and by carefully guided tours of Communist countries.)
9. A conviction that communism is certain to win, and a desire to be on the winning side.
10. A widespread sense of being uprooted, of seeing one's

spiritual and material values disappear. (This state of affairs is most likely to occur after an unsuccessful war. The two greatest victories of communism — in Russia and in China — both followed the devastation and disruption of prolonged war and invasion.)

Exceptions to the Rule

These ten causes do not always explain communism's appeal for some people. For example, it is not always in the poorest countries that the roots of communism strike deep. France is a richer country than Ireland, yet Communists are influential in France but scarcely exist in Ireland. The explanation may be that life in Ireland is comparatively tranquil and stable as contrasted with the tumult in France in recent decades, resulting from foreign invasion and occupation, infiltration, a succession of crises in Algeria, and other disturbing events.

Nor would it be accurate to assume that Communists belong only to the underprivileged groups of the population. In the United States, communism has drawn more support from the fairly well-to-do and the professions than from the poorer groups, such as sharecroppers and migratory farm laborers. Industrial workers, on the other hand — the class on which communism originally placed its greatest hopes of support — have taken the lead in anti-Communist demonstrations in the United States.

Thus it is apparent that people who become Communists do so for a variety of reasons. Let us now take a look at the two great Communist revolutions and see how they attracted their followers.

Russia's Vulnerability

Tsarist Russia was especially vulnerable to violent social revolution because it was less advanced than the rest of Europe, though far ahead of Asia, in its social, economic,

154

and educational development. There were extremes of wealth and poverty rooted in the old Russian system of landowning nobility and peasant serfs. Even the emancipation of the serfs by Tsar Alexander II, in 1861, did not make the serf the equal of the landlord in education, wealth, and opportunity. Although the majority of the peasants did not understand Marxism, they could easily be won over to a program of avenging old wrongs and dividing the big estates among themselves.

Other Russians who were ready for revolution were the industrial workers, who toiled long hours under difficult conditions for little pay. In other countries there had been steady improvement in the workers' situation as new ma-

Weary Russian soldiers taken prisoner outside Warsaw wait to be transported deep behind German lines in World War I.

chines increased productivity and reduced hard labor. But since industrial development did not start in Russia until the end of the 19th century, productivity and wages lagged behind U.S. and Western European standards. Thus Russian workers as a class were more susceptible to revolutionary propaganda.

Another factor that accounted for the appeal of communism in Russia was the absolute power of the tsars. The impossibility, under the tsarist system, of bringing about needed reforms through peaceful *evolutionary* means forced Russian intellectuals, and others who desired political and social change, to advocate extreme *revolutionary* methods.

Still another contributing factor in the revolutionary trend was the discrimination practiced by the Russian autocracy against Poles, Lithuanians, and other non-Russian peoples. The resulting widespread discontent among the affected groups made them more ready to accept revolution as the means of correcting this evil.

Finally, World War I disrupted everyday life and brought suffering to the Russian population. The last prop to the old way of life was removed with the overthrow of the tsars, who had been the symbol of authority for centuries. The well-meaning but rather weak liberals and moderate Socialists who held power for the few months between the downfall of the Tsar and the coming of the Communists could not control the tides of upheaval that were playing into Lenin's hands.

The chief cause of Lenin's support was the war weariness of the Russian people. Many who supported the Bolsheviks did so because they wanted the war to end and because they did not anticipate the ultimate goals of the Russian Bolshevik Party, which could be achieved only by making war against the majority of the Russian population, notably the peasants.

For centuries the Chinese have suffered periodic famine. In the 1960's drought, plus regimentation and inefficiency under the Communist regime, has aggravated the situation.

How the Communists Came to Power in China

The Chinese Revolution took place in a country devastated by war (see Chapter 10). The people lived with the threat of recurrent famines. Poverty and want were so widespread as to be indescribable. The first condition for a climate sympathetic to communism was met: poverty with no hope of improvement. Another condition that existed on every side was illiteracy. The uneducated peasant was a ready subject for mass indoctrination with slogans and promises. To him, any change was an improvement. The government was fluid; for centuries the peasant had owed his allegiance to whatever warlord or other local authority happened to be in power

157

at the moment. So he accepted the gun and the bowl of rice and followed the Communist organizer.

Communism in the West

In both France and Italy, the old "class-war" antagonisms seem to account for the persistence of Communist strength. It has been fashionable among intellectuals in both countries to strike a strong antigovernment pose, regardless of the government in power. In addition, there is the "protest" vote by non-Communists who, for one reason or another, are displeased with their government. However, the growing prosperity of Europe has largely weakened the prospect of a Communist attempt to seize power by violence.

In Great Britain a small, hard core of Communists retains influence within some of the trade unions, but it has been a long time since the British Communists have mustered strength enough to elect even a single member of Parliament.

In the United States, Communists are even more isolated from national life than they are in Britain (see Chapter 11).

Why do some individual Americans become Communists or active defenders of the Communist cause? Acute poverty, which does not exist in the United States on a large scale, is seldom the answer. One must seek further, and the reasons are varied. For young people there may be a sense of novelty and adventure, a feeling of challenging established conventions. Sometimes the intense fellowship of a Communist or near-Communist group temporarily meets the needs of a lonely and psychologically uprooted individual. He may require assurance that communism is in a position to supply all the answers. Other persons who dream of a utopian society like to believe that such a society exists in the Soviet Union or China, or both. Dissatisfaction with some aspect of life in the United States may be another motivating cause for the individual who is unable to make a logical point-by-point comparison with conditions in Communist countries.

In any country, historical events are closely connected with a person's decision to join the Communist Party. For example, there is obviously a great difference between the motives which impel people to become Communists before and after the rule of the Communist Party is established. In Russia before 1917, a revolutionary faced prison and exile if he fell into the hands of the police. In China, in certain areas and at certain times, death was the penalty for Communist activity. Persons who joined the Communist Party under such circumstances were ready to face severe consequences for their convictions. But once the Communist Party is in power, this picture changes radically. Then membership in the Party is the road to power and privilege. Personal ambition — for a better job, for political influence, for social advantages — rather than idealism, is likely to dictate application for membership.

In non-Communist countries, on the other hand, changing world and domestic conditions cause the popularity of communism to fluctuate. For example, in the 1930's the appeal of communism rose as idealistic young men from the Western democracies rushed to Spain to help the Loyalist cause, which was also supported by the Communists. At home, lengthening bread lines and the pinch of unemployment caused some educated people to seek in communism an answer to America's economic problems.

Postwar Soviet expansion disillusioned many potential sympathizers. The appeal of communism hit an all-time low in 1956 with the publication of Khrushchev's secret report outlining the bloody crimes of the Soviet state under Stalin and the suppression of the Hungarian popular uprising. These events were followed by some desertions of disillusioned intellectuals from the Communist parties of the West.

And so to the question, "Why do people become Communists?" the answers are almost as varied as the number of people concerned and the times and places in which they live.

CHAPTER 12 — STUDY AIDS

Words and Names to Understand

sharecroppers   "class war"   Loyalist

Checkup Questions

1. What U.S. groups have tended to support communism?
2. Why are the Communists more influential in France than in Ireland?
3. For what reasons do some Americans become Communists?
4. Why did many Americans leave the Communist Party in 1956?
5. With what particular group in Great Britain have Communists retained some influence?

Questions to Think About

1. Which causes given for the appeal of communism to some people seem to be most important? Give reasons to support your answer.
2. Why have industrial workers in the United States often taken the lead in anti-Communist demonstrations?
3. Why are Soviet leaders so concerned about the growing prosperity of Europe?
4. Why is education such an important weapon against communism?

Books, Pamphlets, and Articles to Read

Paperback Books:

Bell, Oliver, *The Two Chinas.* Scholastic, 1962; Ch. 4.
Crossman, Richard, ed., *The God That Failed.* Bantam.
Khrushchev, Nikita, *Anatomy of Terror.* Public Affairs Press, 1956.
Weingast, David E., *This Is Communism.* Oxford, 1961; Ch. 8.

Other Books:

Barghoorn, Frederick C., *Soviet Cultural Offensive.* Princeton University Press, 1960.
Chambers, Whittaker, *Witness.* Random House, 1952.
Gouzenko, Igor, *The Iron Curtain.* Dutton, 1948.
Kravchenko, Victor, *I Chose Freedom.* Scribner, 1946.

Articles:

"Challenge of the 'New Soviet Man,' " Urie Bronfenbrenner, *New York Times Magazine,* Aug. 27, 1961.
"The Communist Party, USA," Harold H. Martin. *Saturday Evening Post,* May 19, 1962.
"An Editor Reports on Europe and Russia," Gardner Cowles. *Look,* June 5, 1962.
"Utopia for Export." *New Republic,* Aug. 21, 1961.

The Might of Communism

The anxiety of the people of the Free World over the possibility of a nuclear war is based not on the fear that the United States will start such a war, but that the Soviet Union will; or that Communist China will, when that government comes into possession of nuclear arms; or that a nuclear war may be triggered by accident, through a mistaken report or wrong interpretation of a report.

In 1946, when the United States was still the sole possessor of the A-bomb, the U.S. government offered a plan to the United Nations for international control of atomic energy. It was willing to surrender its atomic secrets to an international authority, provided the U.S.S.R. would agree to outlaw the A-bomb. The proposal was approved by all members of the U.N., but rejected by the Soviet bloc.

The Soviet leaders at that time knew full well, as they do today, that the United States would not start a nuclear war. But the people of the Soviet Union, Red China, and the Communist satellite nations are told that U.S. leaders are warmongers and a threat to world peace.

It has been pointed out in earlier chapters how the Soviet Union and Red China reach out with every means, including the threat and use of force, to draw small independent nations into the Communist network. You have seen how the Soviet Union, through sheer military power, holds Hungary, Poland, Bulgaria, and other once independent nations in its grip; and how Communist agents operate on a world-wide scale in an effort to undermine independent nations and prepare them for a Communist take-over. (It has happened only 90 miles from the U.S. mainland — in Cuba.)

Elements of Communist Strength

In view of what has happened, and is happening in places like Berlin, Laos, and South Vietnam, it is folly to underestimate the power of international communism. Strength enables communism to keep a firm grip on a large part of Eurasia. It is a strength that arises out of the totalitarian nature of a government that has the weapons to compel its people to do what the self-appointed rulers demand of them. This is quite a different kind of strength from that of a democracy, where the people are recognized as individuals, with rights guaranteed by law, including the right to express their will by speech, writing, and ballot.

What is it that gives Soviet and Chinese communism power over so many people? Here are seven of the main elements of Communist strength:

1. *Suppression of Dissent or Resistance.* With its intensive development of the twin instruments of propaganda and terror, communism is a system of rule that is very difficult to shake off. To say that a people discontented with communism can rid themselves of it and try something else makes about as much sense as to say that an animal caught in a steel trap is there of its own volition. There can be no organized resistance when almost everyone is forced to spy on almost everyone else.

162

Rockets on display in November 7, 1963, Soviet anniversary parade.

2. *A Workable Economic System.* Soviet communism in its present form — with its free use of capitalist incentives, piece-work methods of payment, differential wages, bonuses for those executives who achieve high output — has proved a workable economic system. There is no reason to expect that it will collapse from sheer incompetence. But it is important to remember that communism — in the sense of equal pay, equal sharing of everything — is not practiced in any Communist-ruled country at the present time.

3. *Control of War Potential.* Soviet or Chinese communism is well adapted to the preparation and implementation of war. The individual peasant or factory worker in the Soviet Union and China is pushed to the limit of his endurance. There are no free trade unions to defend him against intolerable working conditions and excessive demands on his working capacity. Nor is the government under any compul-

sion to consider the needs of the individual as a consumer, since it directs the production of goods most needed to carry out its domestic and foreign policies.

The Communist economy is a militarist's dream. It makes possible a tremendous concentration of national effort on military goals and the swift development of the heavy industries. It also makes possible the use of the best-qualified scientists in research for nuclear development, missile improvement, and other projects. In free societies, capable scientists may leave the government service because they are offered higher salaries in private industries, or because they prefer to work for pure science. Scientists in Communist countries do not have this freedom.

According to the most reliable estimates, Soviet industrial output, formerly showing impressive annual gains, has been slipping back to a growth rate lower than our own. In total, it is still less than half of that in the United States. But Soviet expenditures on preparations for war are probably higher than comparable U.S. expenditures.

4. *Control of Public Opinion.* In the rough game of power politics, there are practical advantages in being able to move swiftly and to reverse course without warning. Democratic governments cannot get out of step with public opinion in their countries, and public opinion is often slow to change and make adjustments to new dangers. But in Communist-ruled countries public opinion is what the government says it ought to be. The only mass demonstrations are those that the government itself organizes. Hostile Soviet propaganda against a foreign nation is like a faucet: it can be turned on and off at will.

5. *Suppression of Complaints.* Behind the Iron Curtain little criticism is uttered in public. Citizens of Moscow or Peking may make jokes in public about the long lines at the stores or the inferior quality of overcoats, but it is most unlikely that they will complain publicly about the burden of

164

armament, or the horrors of war. There are no sitdowns at rocket-launching sites, no drawn-out discussions about fall-out shelters. The consequent outward calm that appears to characterize Communist countries gives the impression that their citizens are more closely united than those of the Free World, where national policies are openly criticized, where strikes may occur in defense industries, and where industrialists some times disagree with government officials.

6. *Defense in Secrecy.* Secrecy, which is second nature to a Communist government, serves as a military advantage. Soviet military authorities can easily locate America's well-known rocket-launching sites, nuclear reactors, and missile bases on any map, but we do not know anything about the names or location of Soviet bases. These are never mentioned in Soviet newspapers and magazines.

The Communist empire, stretching from the Pacific Ocean to the River Elbe, is for the most part an uncharted area about which little information is given out. It is far harder to penetrate Soviet than American security measures. The rest of the world does not actually know the exact location from which the Soviet cosmonauts Titov and Gagarin were launched into space, nor where they landed. This is in sharp contrast to America's Project Mercury at Cape Kennedy, launching U.S. astronauts for all to see.

7. *Emotional Appeal.* Finally, communism seems to fill a psychological need for many people by filling their days with meetings, special study courses, rallies, social events, and other activities. It claims to give purpose to their lives by solving all their problems: social, economic, and personal.

Communism may appeal to some persons who are socially maladjusted or who lack self-confidence and are perhaps afraid of freedom. Such individuals often gain confidence and a feeling of worth from being told what to do. Communist agents frequently take advantage of weak individuals in other countries and persuade them to acts of espionage.

Weaknesses in the Communist System

It would create a false impression, however, to list these elements of strength without pointing out some offsetting weaknesses of communism:

1. *Exodus from Communist Countries*. In spite of the strict controls in Communist-ruled countries through government regulation of newspapers, radio, TV, and other means of communication, and in spite of secret informers and a strong secret police organization, many persons living in such countries do not accept communism. For proof, one needs only to look at the mass flights of refugees: from East Germany to West Germany, from North Korea to South Korea, from Red

Hong Kong residents pass food to refugees from China. Because colony is overcrowded, they are being sent back home.
WIDE WORLD

China to Hong Kong and Taiwan, from Hungary after the 1956 rebellion, from Russia itself after the 1917 Revolution and during World War II. These mass flights speak too clearly to be misunderstood.

2. *Distrust of the People.* One of the very strengths of the Communist system contains an inherent weakness. It has been pointed out that persons under Communist rule are not likely to disagree openly with government policy. They may fear imprisonment, loss of job, perhaps transfer to another part of the country. When there is no safety valve permitting persons to express their opinions honestly and frankly, there is also no certainty on the part of the government officials as to how popular their regime really is. This uncertainty is reflected in the nervous fear which Soviet authorities show in eliminating politically critical books from foreign exhibitions in Moscow, in limiting social contacts between Russians and foreigners, in forbidding the sale of non-Communist foreign newspapers and jamming foreign radio broadcasts, and in censoring their own newspapers, radio, and other media.

3. *Isolation from Other Societies.* The deliberate isolation of peoples under Communist rule from all but the most limited contact with free countries carries its penalties. Free societies have always been more progressive than others in promoting the well-being of their citizens, economically and socially. Just as a person who reaches out to individuals around him enriches not only his own life but the lives of others, so does a society which reaches beyond itself to help other societies promote its own development and growth.

4. *No Constitutional Succession.* A glaring fault of communism is its basic lack of what might be called "political legitimacy." In free countries, big issues are decided in free elections, and there is a constitution that prescribes what is to happen if the chief executive is suddenly removed from office by death or accident. Communist-ruled countries have no such machinery for free elections. The question of who is to take the dictator's place can be decided only by a free-

Visitors examine a book collection (previously thinned out by Soviet officials) at the U.S. Exhibition, one of the rare times Russians have had access to Western publications.

for-all in the top ranks of the Communist Party. As has been shown, months or years may elapse before the new dictator takes over. The decision may involve a struggle between the army and the police, the mysterious disappearances or public execution of high officials, and shake-ups in all departments of the government. The period of change-over creates uncertainty among the people and may cause even more reversals in foreign policy than usual.

Soviet Economic Goals

At the Communist Party Congress in October, 1961, Premier Khrushchev declared that by 1980 the Soviet Union would be producing 250,000,000 tons of steel per year (its present production is about 70,000,000 tons) and 50 per cent more electrical power than all other countries now generate. He further claimed that by then the gross national product (all goods and services produced in a year) will have increased five times, industrial production six times, and total farm output three and a half times. Soviet industry, he said, will produce nearly twice as many industrial goods as are now turned out in the whole non-Communist world, thereby giving the Soviets the world's highest standard of living.

Such sweeping claims for a distant target date are obviously hard to verify. Soviet plans and goals have frequently been revised in the past. They were revised again in December, 1963, when Khrushchev announced a new 7-year, $46,000,000,000 capital investment program which stressed the expansion of the chemical industry in order to double farm output in 1970. Under this new program, Khrushchev had to lower his sights on production goals of consumer goods as set for 1970 only two years before. Meat, milk, cotton cloth, shoes, and housing production will be less than called for in the earlier plans.

According to recent estimates, Soviet production is between 45 and 50 per cent of the U.S. total. This proportion, however, does not follow through in everything. Soviet output of such things as automobiles, telephones, and television sets is negligible as compared with American or Western European totals. On the other hand, Soviet military production is probably equal to or greater than America's.

The economic status of the Soviet Union in 1980 will depend as much on what happens in the non-Communist countries as on its success in meeting these high goals of output and worker productivity. Khrushchev's calculations may all be upset if the United States and Western Europe — the latter under the stimulus of the Common Market (see page 181) — move ahead rapidly during the next two decades.

Achilles' Heel of Red Economy

The present development of natural resources and production of durable goods in the U.S.S.R. and, to a lesser extent, Red China, represents a distinct asset in terms of military

A tube-rolling mill in Dniepropetrovsk, in western Russia.

power. But neither the Soviet Union nor Communist China has created a general standard of living that would seem desirable or even tolerable to most people in Western Europe and North America.

Indeed, agriculture may be called the Achilles' heel of all Communist economies. The Soviet Union has apparently not been giving China any help with grain or other foodstuffs.

In June, 1962, in the wake of serious food shortages, the Soviet government announced sharp increases in the prices of meat and butter. As usual, blame was placed on the West. Khrushchev said that since the United States was engaged in an arms race and "harboring plans for a surprise nuclear attack on the Soviet Union," it was impossible for the U.S.S.R. to divert funds needed for agriculture from defense and heavy industry. What he did not say was that Communist priority given to guns over butter — here applied literally and dramatically — exposed again to the world a self-imposed weakness in the Soviet economy. In 1963, Soviet grain crop failure (20 per cent below the 1962 level) forced purchases abroad of around one billion dollars' worth of wheat and other feed grains.

ANDERS IN SVENSKA DAZBLADET, STOCKHOLM

Lettering on building: "Khrushchev's meat-processing company."

CHAPTER 13 — STUDY AIDS

Words and Names to Understand

Eurasia   power politics   gross national product
piecework   "political legitimacy"   Common Market

Checkup Questions

1. Why is it so difficult to organize resistance to communism in Communist countries?
2. What capitalistic devices do the Communists use to make their economic system workable?
3. Are free societies or Communist societies more easily organized for war? Give reasons to support your answer.
4. How does the Soviet industrial output compare with that of the U.S.?
5. What evidence is there that many people living under Communist rule do not accept it?

Questions to Think About

1. Why is secrecy so important to a Communist government?
2. How might the Common Market affect Khrushchev's economic goals?
3. How does communism seem to fill a "psychological need" for many?
4. To what extent can the weaknesses of a Communist system be considered strengths in a free society?

Books, Pamphlets, and Articles to Read

Paperback Books:

Cronyn, George. *A Primer on Communism.* Dutton, 1961; Ch. 14.
Jessup, John K., and editors of *Life. Communism; The Nature of Your Enemy.* Time, Inc., 1962; pp. 39-61.
Schwartz, Harry, ed., *The Many Faces of Communism.* Berkley, 1962; Ch. 3.
Djilas, Milovan, *The New Class.* Praeger, 1957; pp. 124-163.

Articles:

"After Khrushchev — Who? What? How?" Max Frankel. *New York Times Magazine,* March 4, 1962.
"Current Documents: Text of the Third Draft Program of the C.P.S.U." *Current History,* Nov., 1961.
"How the Russians Wage Political Warfare," Edmond Taylor. *The Reporter,* May 10, 1962.
"The Price of Soviet Industrialization," Naum Jasny. *Current History,* Nov., 1961.
"World Communism: Phase III," Branko Lazitch. *National Review,* March 13, 1962.

14

The Free World's Response

The Communists, as we have seen, are applying constant pressures against the Free World. Some of these pressures are subtle and sophisticated; others are crude and belligerent. Taken together, they add up to a many-sided challenge — one of the most serious the Western world has ever faced. The challenge posed by the Communists falls into five principal areas:

1. The challenge of communism as a doctrine
2. The challenge of a great military power
3. The challenge of economic competition
4. The challenge of propaganda
5. The challenge of infiltration and subversion

The Free World's greatest task is to meet these challenges and respond to them effectively.

Source of National Strength

Even a society where ideal justice prevailed would not be able to check the onward march of communism if it let down its military defenses. (Recall the fate of Czechoslovakia, a model democracy patterned on our own constitution, which in 1948 fell victim to Soviet threats of force.)

Ideas are properly met by ideas. But tanks and airplanes and bombs and rockets can be withstood only by equal or superior weapons. The first condition of remaining free is to remain strong — militarily, morally, economically.

Ignorance of the nature of communism can only help the Communists. The ideas of Marx and Lenin, as modified and applied by Stalin, Khrushchev, and Mao, should be carefully studied. An understanding of these ideas will help the student see both the weak and strong points of the Communist doctrine. From such knowledge is born strength.

At the same time, our schools and colleges should never allow it to be forgotten that before the Soviet Revolution, before the French Revolution, there was an American Revolution, and that the basic ideals of our Founding Fathers are a living heritage.

Among these ideals — proclaimed in flaming rhetoric in the Declaration of Independence, analyzed in careful detail in the *Federalist Papers,* spelled out with precision in the American Constitution — the following may be listed as primary:

- All legitimate power derives from the consent of the governed.
- There are certain inalienable rights which neither the executive, nor the legislative, nor the judicial branch of the government may abolish.
- Instruments of government should be so devised that no individual and no institution may acquire predominant power.
- The powers of government should be limited and divided.
- There should be a careful balancing and distribution of authority between the federal government and the states.

Need for Courage and Unity

Two very important elements in the struggle to remain free from Communist domination are courage and unity.

Communist diplomacy, like Nazi diplomacy in the past, employs methods of intimidation and blackmail. Soviet advances in rocketry have placed in the hands of Nikita Khrushchev what he regards as a useful instrument of intimidation. As early as the Suez crisis of 1956, the Soviet government, in notes to Great Britain and France, began to threaten London and Paris with obliteration.

Since that time Khrushchev has repeatedly, in public and in private, threatened to use rockets and missiles against countries that do not bow to his will.

Late in the summer of 1958, when Red China began its heavy bombardment of the offshore islands of Quemoy and Matsu, Khrushchev came out in support of his Chinese allies. He dispatched a note to the U.S. government so offensive and threatening in tone that President Eisenhower refused to accept it. This crisis was handled very coolly and realistically, in line with President Eisenhower's declaration to the American people that "There will be no appeasement. I do not think there will be any war." As it developed, there was no withdrawal from Quemoy — and there was no war.

Twice Khrushchev has sought to force a Western retreat and surrender on the issue of West Berlin by setting a time limit for concluding a peace treaty with his own puppet regime in East Germany. One of these time limits was May 29, 1959; the other was December 31, 1961. On both occasions he backed away when he met firm resistance. To be sure, he did authorize the walling off of East Berlin from the rest of the city on August 13, 1961, and has not withdrawn formally from his position that Western troops should leave West Berlin. If his proposal were followed, West Berlin would be transformed into a "demilitarized free city," severing all connections with West Germany.

The North Atlantic Treaty Organization brings together men of many countries. Here troops from Belgium, Luxembourg, and Holland train during NATO maneuvers in Belgium.

Both the Western powers and the West Berliners regard this as a thinly disguised scheme to bring West Berlin — where at least 98 per cent of the people, according to the election returns, are opposed to communism — under the domination of Communist-ruled East Germany.

The United States, in agreement with the leaders of Britain and France, has taken a firm stand on maintaining the political independence of West Berlin and the right of the Western powers to keep their troops there and enjoy free access to the city.

In the summer of 1961 Khrushchev threatened to blow up

the Acropolis if Greece remained loyal to its obligations under the North Atlantic Treaty Organization. The Greek Premier, Constantin Karamanlis, replied that although the Soviet Union might have the physical force to destroy the Acropolis, it could never destroy the ideas of liberty for which the Acropolis stood.

Though Khrushchev apparently regards such threats as a normal means of carrying on negotiations, he has been much more moderate since President Kennedy's firm stand in the 1962 Cuba crisis. Still, it would be the beginning of the decline of the West to yield to his threats and make concessions, in the hope of buying peace. History, from the time of Pericles to the time of Hitler, has shown that more often than not appeasement (which may be defined as retreating before force or threat of force) can never lead to peace with honor. It can only lead to war with dishonor. Thus steadfast courage must be the first imperative of the West in facing the aggressive thrust of communism, whether this thrust comes from Moscow or from Peking.

The second imperative is a maximum degree of unity — political, military, economic, and moral — among the anti-Communist powers. The Soviet leaders — Lenin, Stalin, and now Khrushchev — have demonstrated their belief in and their mastery of a very old practice of statecraft: divide and rule. To try to take advantage of differences among adversaries, to make an appeal to one non-Communist government and a diametrically different appeal to another — this is the very essence of the Soviet diplomatic offensive.

Complete unity in the West is still far from a reality. Disagreements among the Western Allies, arising from differences in national interests and from conflicting views as to the best tactical approach to the problem in hand, continue to crop up. Yet, looking back over the past 15 years, we see encouraging signs of progress toward military and economic unity in the community of anti-Communist nations.

A U.S. Marine captain (right) shows South Vietnamese marines how to use a flame thrower in exercises held near Saigon. Vietnamese soldiers are in camouflaged uniforms.

The Military Response

Since the end of World War II, Free World nations have united in a number of pacts designed to serve as a barrier against Communist expansion. One of the strongest and most effective of these alliances is the North Atlantic Treaty Organization (NATO). Set up in 1949 to provide for a mutual defense against an aggressive Communist system, it is now a 16-nation pact among all Western European countries outside the Iron Curtain, except for Spain and four neutral powers: Switzerland, Sweden, Austria, and Ireland.

The United States, reversing the stand it took after World War I, is now fully committed to the defense of Europe. Some of the best U.S. combat units are maintained in Germany. Following their experience in the last war, such former European neutrals as Belgium and the Netherlands, Denmark and Norway, have decided that collective security through a defensive alliance offers a better prospect than an attitude of neutrality. Accordingly, these countries too have joined NATO.

Checked by NATO in Europe, the Communists eyed Southeast Asia for new conquests in the early 1950's. Communist guerrillas spread terror in rubber-rich Malaya. In 1951 the Chinese Communists took over Tibet and put pressure on Burma and Laos. In 1954 the Communists swept into power in North Vietnam, after defeating the French colonial rulers.

Faced with Communist penetration into Southeast Asia, the United States joined with Australia, New Zealand, Pakistan, the Philippines, Thailand, Britain, and France to form the Southeast Asia Treaty Organization (SEATO) in 1954. Three other Southeast Asian nations — South Vietnam, Cambodia, and Laos — are under SEATO protection, although they are not members of the pact. In recent years, the Communists have stepped up their penetration of South Vietnam to the extent that the United States government was compelled to send some 15,000 military advisers and technicians to that country to help the South Vietnamese check further Communist expansion. In addition, the United States has been supplying military and economic aid to South Vietnam at the rate of $500,000,000 a year.

As early as the 1950's, the Soviet Union began making threatening moves in the oil-rich lands of the Middle East. To prevent Communist expansion into this region, Great Britain, Iran, Iraq, Pakistan, and Turkey set up, in 1955, a mutual defense pact called the Middle East Treaty Organization (METO) — also known as the Baghdad Pact.

METO linked with NATO members to the west and SEATO members to the east to form a barrier of anti-Communist nations around much of the Communist bloc.

In 1958, however, a hole was ripped in this barrier. Iraq, whose capital, Baghdad, had been METO headquarters, left the alliance after a revolution that put a neutralist regime in power. METO moved its headquarters to Turkey and became known as the Central Treaty Organization (CENTO).

The United States is not a CENTO member, but cooperates with CENTO in matters of defense. CENTO nations also cooperate to help raise educational and economic standards.

Two other alliances unite Western powers. The Rio Pact was signed in 1947 by the United States and 20 republics of Latin America. Member nations are pledged to aid any other member in the event of an armed attack against one of them. In 1951 the United States, Australia, and New Zealand signed a treaty known as ANZUS (for the initial letters of the three nations), pledging mutual protection against any common danger in the Pacific area.

These alliances form the heart of the Free World's defenses against communism. Much of the muscle for this defense system is supplied by a globe-girdling belt of U.S. bases from which planes and missiles can be ordered into action within minutes.

The Economic Response

As the Free World was arming against communism's aggressive thrusts, it also used many economic weapons to parry the threat from Moscow. It is well to remember that the Communists took over the countries of Romania, Bulgaria, Albania, and Yugoslavia in the years immediately after World War II; Poland and Hungary fell to the Communists in 1947; a year later Czechoslovakia was the victim of a Communist coup. Only three years after World War II, the Iron Curtain had fallen across the heart of Europe.

Fearful that Soviet expansion might engulf the war-weakened nations of Western Europe, the United States embarked on an unprecedented program of aid to its anti-Communist allies.

In 1947, at President Truman's request, the U.S. Congress appropriated $400,000,000 to aid Greece and Turkey in their defense against Communist aggression.

In 1948, U.S. Secretary of State George C. Marshall presented a dramatic plan for aiding European nations. Under the Marshall Plan, vitally needed transfusions of economic aid were poured into the war-shattered countries of West European nations to help them get back on their feet and thereby resist Communist subversion.

The Marshall Plan was administered by an agency known as the ECA (Economic Cooperation Administration). It had a threefold purpose: to stimulate European production, strengthen and stabilize European currency, and promote international trade. As a result of billions of dollars worth of Marshall Plan aid, the West European countries were able to rebuild their economies. Today the area is riding the crest of a surging boom that has brought a spectacular era of prosperity.

In recent years Western Europe has also been moving toward a new economic unity, centering around a core of six nations: West Germany, France, Italy, the Netherlands, Belgium, and Luxembourg. First came the "coal and steel community," under which these six nations abolished among themselves all tariffs on coal and steel. Now they have established a more ambitious project: the European Economic Community, or Common Market.

The goal of the EEC (which came into being January 1, 1958) is to abolish all tariffs among member nations by a gradual process that will be completed by 1970. This will mean a free trade area of 165,000,000 people, the richest common market area in the world, after the United States. Great

Volkswagens roll off an assembly line in Wolfsburg, near the East German border in northern West Germany. Since World War II, Volkswagen has built more than 4,000,000 vehicles.

Britain applied for membership in 1961, but France blocked her immediate entry. France insisted on certain changes in Britain's economic relations with the Commonwealth countries and the United States. These terms were unacceptable to the British. Meantime, six other countries (Norway, Denmark, Sweden, Switzerland, Austria, and Portugal) announced that they too would seek to associate with the EEC.

The Propaganda Response

The battle to influence people and win friends is also one of words. Some persons tend to think, incorrectly, of "propaganda" as something that is false. Actually, propaganda is information released by a government or an organization for the purpose of presenting its official point of view.

American propaganda assumes various forms in the continuing battle of words with the Communist nations. It is centered in three large groups — one an official U.S. government agency, the others sponsored by private organizations. The official agency is the U.S. Information Agency. It employs experienced journalists, public relations representatives, and other specialists working in the United States and abroad. They maintain libraries and information centers in foreign countries and supply foreign newspapers with news, photographs, and printed material concerning life in the United States. The U.S.I.A. also sponsors Voice of America radio broadcasts. "Voice" transmissions are beamed throughout the world, though they are not heard inside the United States.

The two private agencies engaged in the propaganda battle are Radio Free Europe, which transmits programs to the Soviet satellites (with the exception of East Germany), and Radio Liberty, which beams programs to the Soviet Union. Radio Liberty uses Russian and 16 other languages spoken in the U.S.S.R. It is on the air 24 hours a day, using 17 transmitters located in Western Europe and Taiwan to send its programs, which are planned and prepared in Munich, New York, and Taipei.

These stations — and the Voice of America — present taped programs of events originating in the United States and other Western democracies, and broadcasts by former citizens of Communist countries who speak directly to the people, in their native tongues. Such broadcasts may include religious services, presentation of musical or literary programs, dramatic presentations, and sports. All are based on presenting the facts about events inside and outside the Communist

Of Radio Liberty's 400 announcers, script writers, and other employees, 200 once resided in what is now the Soviet Union.

countries, using both news accounts and political commentary. Communist censorship often keeps the facts from the people, or distorts them.

Infiltration and Subversion

Communism menaces the Free World on still other fronts. The Soviet Union extends its influence throughout the world through a network of over 90 Communist parties, including one in the United States. In countries where it is outlawed, the Communist Party operates underground. Each party receives instructions from Moscow or Peking for its program of action.

The work of the Communist parties in foreign countries is supplemented by the activities of Soviet agents, whose task it is to undermine free democratic institutions and to provoke disturbances and riots. When the political climate is favorable, they may incite an armed insurrection, leading to the ultimate replacement of a local government by a Communist regime.

Thus, vigilance against Communists who may be countrymen is still another necessity in this Cold War age.

Democracy at Home

Answering the challenge of communism abroad is important, but the nations of the Free World also have the responsibility of guarding democracy at home.

It is assumed that one of the most effective ways of opposing communism is to create an ever better social order within free societies. But this is the aim of a free society under any circumstances. However, it is unfortunate that some people are prone to interpret this course too literally, asserting that we have no right to resist communism until and unless we have created a perfect society in our own country. This contention is clearly absurd.

Ideal conditions do not exist anywhere in the world. Even in the United States and France, with their strong traditions of liberty and equality, and in Great Britain, where the freedom of the individual has been upheld for centuries, discrimination and prejudice still exist. But the basic freedoms of voting, speech, press, and assembly will ultimately make it possible to eliminate such abuses and defects without resort to violence.

Communism, in its brutality and insensitivity to human rights and liberties, has given the peoples under its rule no such freedom to correct its built-in abuses. Under Communist rule—where there are no free elections, or free press, or free speech—prospects for peaceful change and reform are at best very difficult and uncertain. Therein lies a basic criticism of communism as a political system.

CHAPTER 14 — STUDY AIDS

Words and Names to Understand

SEATO	CENTO	Marshall Plan
NATO	Rio Pact	Common Market
METO	ANZUS	

Checkup Questions

1. What five areas of challenge are posed by communism?
2. What are the primary ideals of our free society?
3. How has Khrushchev used intimidation as a means of diplomacy?
4. What organizations were formed to prevent Communist expansion?
5. What is the purpose of the newly formed Common Market?
6. Describe the operation of such agencies as Radio Free Europe, Radio Liberty, and the United States Information Agency.

Questions to Think About

1. How effective have the Communists' "divide and rule" tactics been?
2. What factors have caused the United States to reverse its former policy of isolation?
3. Will a successful Common Market benefit the Free World? Give reasons for your answer.
4. How might the free nations best combat Communist propaganda?

Books, Pamphlets, and Articles to Read

Paperback Books:

Cronyn, George. *A Primer of Communism.* Dutton, 1961; Chs. 15 and 16.

Fearey, Robert A., *The U.S. versus the U.S.S.R.* Public Affairs Press, 1959; pp. 19-37.

Weingast, David, *This Is Communism.* Oxford, 1961; Ch. 10.

Articles:

"Asia Puts Some Sharp Questions to Us," Saul Padover. *New York Times Magazine,* March 4, 1962.

"A Direction for the West," Barbara Ward. *Saturday Review,* Jan. 27, 1962.

"Eventually 'Public Opinion' Prevails," Louis Halle. *New York Times Magazine,* Oct. 15, 1961.

"Myth of 'Triumphant Communism,'" Harlan Cleveland. *New York Times Magazine,* Nov. 5, 1961.

"The Communist Dread of the Common Market," Madeleine and Marvin Kalb. *The Reporter,* July 19, 1962.

"The Soviet Challenge and Our Response," Anthony T. Bauscaren. *Vital Speeches,* Apr. 15, 1962.

"The West's Citizen-Diplomats," Elmo Roper. *Saturday Review,* Jan. 6, 1962.

A Chronology of Communism

1848	Marx and Engels publish *The Communist Manifesto*
1864	Marx helps organize the First International
1867	Marx publishes Volume 1 of *Das Kapital*
1889	Followers of Marx organize the Second International
1903	Russian Social Democratic Party split into two groups: Bolsheviks (led by Lenin) and Mensheviks
1914-1917	Russia suffers heavy defeat in World War I
1917	Tsar Nicholas II of Russia gives up his throne
1917	Bolsheviks seize control of Russia's capital
1918-1920	Civil war in Russia
1919	Lenin sets up the Comintern (Third International)
1919	U.S. Communist Party organized
1921	Lenin starts the New Economic Policy (NEP)
1921	Chinese Communist Party organized
1922	Union of Soviet Socialist Republics organized
1924	Death of Lenin
1927	Chiang Kai-shek expels Soviet advisers from China
1928	Collectivization and First Five-Year Plan initiated in U.S.S.R.
1933	United States recognizes Soviet Union's Communist regime
1935-1939	Stalin's purges
1939	Soviet Union and Nazi Germany sign nonaggression pact
1939-1940	Soviet Union takes over parts of Poland and Finland; also Estonia, Latvia, Lithuania, and northern Romania
1940	Trotsky murdered in Mexico
1941	Nazi Germany invades Soviet Union
1942-1943	U.S.S.R. armies defeat Germans at Stalingrad
1945	Yalta Conference (Stalin, Roosevelt, Churchill) in Soviet Union
1945-1948	Soviets impose Communist rule on eight East European nations
1948	Tito-Stalin break (first split between Communist nations)
1948-1949	Soviet blockade of West Berlin
1949	Communists conquer China mainland
1949	Soviet Union explodes its first atomic bomb
1950-1953	Korean War
1953	Death of Stalin
1953	Revolt in East Germany crushed by Soviet troops
1955	U.S.S.R. and satellites set up Warsaw Pact
1956	Khrushchev denounces Stalin at 20th Communist Party Congress
1956	Hungarian rebellion crushed by Soviet troops
1957	U.S.S.R. orbits first man-made satellite
1957	Khrushchev removes from power his chief rivals for leadership
1961	Communist-built wall divides Berlin
1962	Crisis over Soviet missiles in Cuba
1962	Dispute between Soviet Union and Communist China deepens
1963	Partial nuclear test-ban treaty signed

Pronunciation Guide

The pronunciation of difficult words in the text is given in parentheses following the entries below. The system followed here uses only one diacritical mark and translates each syllable into the nearest common English equivalent. Syllables set in capitals are accented. If the whole word is in lowercase letters, the stress on each syllable is approximately equal. Principal sound equivalents: *ay* (as in ale); *a* (as in cat); *ah* (as in arm); *uh* (unaccented *a* as in sofa); *ch* (as in chair); *ee* (as in eat); *eh* (as in end); *g* (as in go); *ih* (as in ill); *ie* (as in pie); *j* (as in joke); *k* (as in keep); *oh* (as in old); *ah* (as in odd); *aw* (as in soft); *oo* (as in food); *ŏŏ* (as in foot); *ow* (as in out); *s* (as in sit); *t* (as in tin); *u* (as in up); *ur* (as in urn); *z* (as in zone).

Adzhubei, Aleksei (ahd-zhoo-BAY, ah-lck-SAY)
Belgrade (BEL-grayd)
Bogdanov (bahg-DAH-nohv)
Bolshevik (BALL-sheh-veek)
bourgeoisie (bŏŏr-zhwah-ZEE)
Borodin, Michael (boh-rah-DEEN)
Brest-Litovsk (brest-lee-TAWVSK)
Buddhist (BŎŎD-ist)
Bukharin, Nikolai (boo-KAH-reen)
Bulganin, Nikolai (bool-GAH-neen)
Chiang Kai-shek (jahng kie-shek)
Chou En-lai (joe en-lie)
coup d'état (koo day-TAH)
Dalai Lama (dah-lie LAH-mah)
Dniepropetrovsk (nyeh-proh-peh-TRAWVSK)
Djilas, Milovan (JEE-lahs, MEE-loh-vahn)
Fuchs, Klaus (fooks, klows)
Gapon, Father (gah-POHN)
Gomulka, Wladyslaw (goh-MOOL-kah, VLAH-dee-slahv)
Hammarskjöld, Dag (HAH-mahr-shuld, dahg)
Hangö (HANG-yoo)
Hegel, Georg (HAY-gel, gay-ORG)
Kadar, Janos (KAH-dahr, YAH-nahsh)
Kaganovich (kah-guh-NOH-veech)
Kamenev (KAH-meh-nyahv)
Karamanlis, Constantin (Kah-rah-mahn-LEES, KAWN-stahn-teen)
Karelia, Isthmus of (kah-REE-lih-ah)
Katyn (kah-TEEN)
Khrushchev, Nikita (kroosh-CHUV, nee-KEE-tah)
Kiev (KEE-yev)
Kirov, Sergei (KEE-ruv, sehr-GAY)
Kolchak, Alexander (kahl-CHAHK)

Kuomintang (gwoh-min-dahng)
Laos (louz)
Lenin (Vladimir Ilyich Ulyanov) (LYEH-neen; vlah-DEE-meer eel-YEECH ool-YAH-nuv)
Liu Shao-chi (lyoo show-gee)
Malenkov, Georgi (MAH-lyen-kohv)
Mao Tse-tung (MAH-oh dzuh-dŏŏng)
Matsu (mah-TSOO)
Mikoyan, Anastas (mee-kuh-YAHN, ah-nah-STAHS)
Molotov, Vyacheslav (MAW-law-tuv, vyah-cheh-SLAHV)
Myasnikov, Gabriel (MYAH-snee-kohv, gah-bree-EL)
Nagy, Imre (nahdj, IM-reh)
Plekhanov, Georgi (plyeh-KAH-nohv)
Pyatakov (pyah-tah-KOHV)
Quemoy (kee-MOY)
Rasputin, Gregory (rahs-POO-teen)
Rhee, Syngman (ree, SING-mahn)
Rokossovsky, Konstantin (ruh-kuh-SAHV-skee, kun-stan-TEEN)
Rykov, Aleksei (rih-KAWV)
Sputnik (SPOOT-neek)
Sun Yat-sen (sŏŏn yaht-sen)
Synod (SIN-ud)
Taipei (tie-pay)
Taiwan (tie-wahn)
Teheran (teh-heh-RAHN)
Thailand (tie-land)
Tito, Josip Broz (TEE-toh, YOH-seep brohz)
tsarist (ZAHR-ist)
Tuva (TOO-vah)
Vietnam (vee-et-NAHM)
Vladivostok (vlah-dee-vah-STAWK)
Wyszynski, Stefan, Cardinal (vih-SHIN-skee, STAY-fahn)
Zinoviev (zee-NAW-vyev)

Index

Adzhubei, Aleksei, 114
Africa, 10, 128
agents, Soviet, 10, 20, 124-125, 152, 162, 184
AGITPROP, 19-20
airlift, West Berlin, 62
Albania, 6, 20, 64, 130, 131, 146, 180
American propaganda, 183-184
American Relief Administration, 40
anti-imperialism, 139
anti-Semitism, 119-120, 139, 156
ANZUS, 180
arms deadlock, 80-82
art, Soviet control of, 13-14, 19-20, 114
Asia, 10, 128, 134, 138, 139, 179
authoritarian government, 13, 14
Baghdad Pact, 179
Beria, Lavrenti, 69, 71
Berlin dispute, 60-64, 77-80, 141, 150, 162, 175-176
Bessarabia, 50, 51
black markets, Soviet, 97
"Bloody Sunday," 29
Bolshevik Party, 29, 33-34, 42, 86, 145, 156
Bolshevik Revolution, 6, 14, 22, 27, 29, 30, 33-34, 42, 43, 84-85, 105, 115, 116, 123, 138, 139, 154-156
books, Soviet control of, 13-14, 19-20, 112-114, 115, 167
Borodin, Michael, 125
brainwashing, 135
Brest-Litovsk, peace conference at, 36
Bukharin, Nikolai, 42, 43, 48
Bulganin, Nikolai, 72
Bulgaria, 6, 51, 64, 139, 146, 162, 180
Burma, 179
Byrnes, James F., 64
Cambodia, 134, 179
capitalism, 23-25, 27, 85
Castro, Fidel, 6, 89
Central Committee, Soviet Communist Party, 15, 16, 76, 112
Central Treaty Organization (CENTO), 180
Chiang Kai-shek, 125-128
China, Communist: and Albania, 6, 20, 130, 131; and India, 132; and Laos, 134, 162, 179; and Nationalist China, 123-128, 139, 156, 158; and North Korea, 6, 20, 67, 132; and

North Vietnam, 6, 20, 134, 179; and Poland, 130; and U.S.S.R., 6, 123-126, 128-131, 150, 171; and Tibet, 6, 132, 179; and U.N., 131-132; and Yugoslavia, 130; controls, 134-135, 162-165; establishment of, 123; flight of refugees from, 166-167; food shortage, 134-135; "Great Leap Forward," 134-135; industrialization, 124, 128-129, 134-135; military power, 132, 134, 169, 171; peasants, 134, 163; satellites, 6; standard of living, 131, 134-135, 171
China, Nationalist: and Communist China, 123-128, 139, 156, 158; and Japan, 126; and U.S., 126-127, 128; and U.S.S.R., 123-126, 150
Chinese Communist Party, 124-125, 138
Chou En-lai, 123
Churchill, Winston, 10, 53-54
Clay, General Lucius D., 62
Cold War, 10, 54, 56-57, 88, 147, 184
collective farms, 17, 19, 43-44, 74-75, 87, 100, 111-112, 139, 171
colonialism, 131, 138, 141, 147
Common Market, 69, 181
communes, 134-135
communications, Soviet control of, 13-14, 19-20, 112-113, 115, 166, 167
communism: and democratic government, 11, 13, 16-17, 162, 164, 185; and freedom, 13-20, 58, 90, 104-121, 138-139, 162-165, 185; appeal of, factors in, 152-159, 165; centers of, 89-90; challenge of, 173; goal of, 16; "primitive," 23; strength of, elements of, 162-165; system of, 13-20; "war," 39-40, 86; weaknesses of, 166-168
Communist Information Bureau (Cominform), 145-146
Communist International (Comintern), 137, 138, 144-145
Communist Manifesto, 22-23, 144
Communist Party: ambition of, 138; Chinese, 124-125, 138; French, 145, 148, 154, 158; Great Britain, 158; Indian, 138; international organization, 143-146; Italian, 145, 148, 158; members of, privileges of, 159; non-Communist countries, 147-148; So-

viet, 14, 16-20, 41, 44, 45-50, 70, 72,
73, 76, 86-87, 112; strategy of, 138;
underground, 20, 184; United States,
20, 147-148, 154, 158, 184
Communist propaganda, 7, 10, 19-20,
58, 90, 108-109, 117, 121, 127-128,
138-141, 153, 161, 162, 164, 171
Communist Revolution, *see* Bolshevik
Revolution
Communist spies, 141-143, 152
Congo crisis, 82
Constituent Assembly, 29, 41-42
cosmonauts, Soviet, 165
Council of Ministers, 17
Council of Nationalities, 17
Council of the Union, 17
Cuba, 6, 82, 89, 148, 162
Czechoslovakia, 6, 60, 139, 145, 146,
173-174, 180
Das Kapital, 24
de Gaulle, General, 148
democratic government, 11, 13, 16-17,
162, 164, 185
Denikin, General Anton, 38
disarmament proposals, 80-82
Djilas, Milovan, 86, 88
"doctor's plot," 70
Dumas, 29, 30, 32
East Berlin, 60-64, 77-80, 150, 175-176
East Germany, 6, 60, 139, 146, 150,
166, 175
Eisenhower, Dwight D., 62, 77-78, 175
Engels, Friedrich, 22
espionage, 141-143, 152
Estonia, 50, 51, 118, 139, 150
European Free Trade Association, 182
F.B.I., 148
Finland, 50, 51, 149
First International, 144
Five-Year plans, 43-44
forced-labor camps, 18, 43, 44, 47, 50,
70
free markets, Soviet, 96-97
freedom: and communism, 13-20, 58,
90, 104-121, 138-139, 162-165, 185;
maintenance of, 175-177; seven tests
of, 10-11
Gapon, Father, 29
Geneva conferences, 77, 81
Georgia, Soviet invasion of, 149
Germany: and Britain, 52, 60; and
Finland, 50, 51; and Poland, 36, 50,
52, 56-57; and U.S.S.R., 30, 33-37,
44, 50-52, 54, 56, 58, 60-64, 77-80,

138-139; partition of, 52-53, 60, 62
Gomulka, Wladyslaw, 73, 75
Gorky, Maxim, 48
Gouzenko, 142
Great Britain: and Germany, 52, 60;
and U.S., 53-54, 81; and U.S.S.R.,
37, 52-54, 81, 150; Communist Par-
ty, 158; Communist spies, 143
Greece, Cold War in, 64-65, 181
guerrilla warfare, 38, 57, 64, 65, 123-
128, 134, 152, 179
Hammarskjöld, Dag, 82
Hegel, Georg, 23
Hitler, Adolf, 51, 52, 54, 138-139, 145,
147, 177
Hungary, 6, 51-52, 75-76, 139, 146,
159, 162, 166-167, 180
"imperialists," 51, 126, 130, 138, 141,
147
India, 132
indoctrination, Communist, 19-20,
104-108, 127, 156
infiltration, Communist, 90, 143, 154
Internal Security Act, 148
International Workers' Association, 144
Iron Curtain, 60, 164, 178-179, 180
Ivan the Terrible, 47
Japan, 29, 37, 54, 58, 126, 142-143
Kadar, Janos, 76
Kaganovich, 76
Kamenev, 42, 48
Katyn massacre, 56
Kennan, George F., 45
Kennedy, President John F., 7, 79, 82,
114, 128, 141, 177
Kerensky, Alexander, 32-34
Khrushchev, Nikita: approved by
Stalin, 70; denounces Stalin, 47-48,
50, 70, 73, 131, 159; dictatorship,
76-82; early life, 70; First Secretary
of Communist Party, 17; peaceful-
coexistence policy, 130, 141; prom-
ises to Russians, 100-102; propagan-
da, 7, 10, 140-141, 171; rise to
power, 69-72, 76-77; threats by, 7,
10, 140, 175-177
Kirov, Sergei, 47
Kolchak, Admiral Alexander, 38
Komsomol, 107-108, 109-111
Korean War, 57, 65-67, 70, 132
Kornilov, General, 33
Kronstadt uprising, 40
Kuomintang, 124-127, 138
Laos, 134, 162, 179

Latin America, 148, 180
Latvia, 50, 51, 118, 139, 149
League of Nations, 50-51
Lenin, Nikolai: and Bolshevik Revolution, 27, 29, 30, 33-34, 42, 84-85, 156; birth, 27; death, 42; denounces Stalin, 42; dictatorship, 33-42, 44, 45; exiles, 27, 31-32; Marxism and, 27-28, 85; purges, 47; tomb, 72
Lithuania, 50, 51, 57, 139, 149
Liu Shao-chi, 130
MacArthur, General Douglas, 67
Malaya, guerrilla warfare in, 179
Malenkov, Georgi, 69, 70, 71, 76
Maleter, Pal, 75-76
Malik, Jacob, 67
Manchuria, 54, 58, 126
Mao Tse-tung, 6, 84, 123-125, 174
Marshall, General George C., 126, 181
Marshall Plan, 60, 146, 181
Marx, Karl, 22-25
Marxism, 23-25, 27-28, 85, 123-124, 143-144, 155, 174
Matsu, 175
Mensheviks, 29, 31-32
METO, 179-180
Mikoyan, Anastas, 73
Mindszenty, Cardinal, 75
Molotov, Vyachevslav, 51, 64, 69, 76
Murrow, Edward R., 183
Myasnikov, Gabriel, 86
Nagy, Imre, 75-76
Nazi-Soviet nonaggression pact, 46, 50-51, 57, 145, 147
Nenni, Pietro, 148
New Economic Policy (NEP), 40-42
Nikolaev, L., 47
North Atlantic Treaty Organization (NATO), 177, 178-179
North Korea, 6, 20, 58, 65-67, 132, 166
North Vietnam, 6, 20, 134, 179
nuclear testing, 80-82, 150
Nuremberg trials, 56
orbital flights, Soviet, 92, 165
Orthodox Church, Russian, 117-118
Pasternak, Boris, 113
peaceful coexistence, 130, 141
Plekhanov, Georgi, 29
Poland: and Communist China, 130; and Germany, 36, 50, 52, 56-57; and U.S.S.R., 6, 38, 44, 50, 52, 53-54, 56-57, 73-74, 130, 139, 146, 150, 162, 180; collective farms, 74-75; guerrilla warfare, 57; industries, 19;

partition of, 50, 150; religion, 118; revolt, 73-74
Poznan riots, 73-74
Potsdam agreement, 53, 60
Presidium, Communist Party, 16, 76
proletariat, dictatorship of, 23-24, 27-28, 85
Quemoy, 175
Radio Free Europe, 183-184
Radio Liberty, 183-184
Rasputin, Gregory, 30
Red Army, 36-38, 48, 138-139, 152
Rhee, Syngman, 65
Riga, treaty signed at, 38
Rio Pact, 180
Rokossovsky, Konstantin, 74
Romania, 6, 50, 51, 139, 146, 180
Romanov dynasty, fall of, 31-32
Roosevelt, Franklin D., 53-54
Rosenberg, Ethel and Julius, 143
Russia (before Revolution), see tsarism
Rykov, Aleksei I., 42, 43, 48
Second International, 144
secret police, 27, 46, 47, 69, 75, 76, 86, 139, 152, 159, 167
Secretariat, Communist Party, 16, 19-20
Shostakovich, Dimitri, 113-114
Siberia, 27, 37, 40, 50, 76
Social Democratic Party, Russian, 27, 29
Social Revolutionaries, 32, 33, 42
socialism, 22, 88, 141, 143-144
Socialist International, 144
Socialist parties, 24, 25, 28, 40, 42, 75, 145, 148, 156
South Korea, 65-67, 132, 166
South Vietnam, 132, 152, 162, 179
Southeast Asia Treaty Organization (SEATO), 179
Soviet Union: and Communist China, 6, 123-126, 128-131, 150, 171; and U.N., 60, 66, 76, 82, 161; and U.S. 44, 52, 53-54, 57-58, 60-64, 77-82, 131, 150; and West Berlin, 7, 62-64, 77-80, 141, 150, 175-176; armament production, 71-72, 76, 96, 100-102, 163-164, 169; art, 13-14, 19-20, 114; civil war, 36-38; consumer goods, 76, 92-98; controls, 13-20, 104-121, 138-139, 149, 162-165, 166; cultural life, 112-115; economic goals, 168-169; economic system, 6, 18-19, 39-40, 43, 163, 169, 171; education, 18-19, 104-108, 139, 141; "elections," 17, 41, 69; entertainment,

13-14, 19-20, 112-115; famine, 40, 43, 44; Five-Year plans, 43-44; food supply, 94, 171; government organization, 16-17; heavy industries, 42-43, 71-72, 96, 100-102, 164, 169; housing problems, 11, 98-100; industrial workers, 26, 33, 124, 155-156; industrialization, 42-43, 71-72, 96, 100-102, 155-156, 164, 168-169; military strength, 6, 132, 169, 171; music, 19-20, 114; peasants, 26, 33, 34, 39, 40, 42, 85, 86, 96, 139, 155, 163; physical fitness program, 110-112; population, 16; religion, 18-19, 115-121; satellites, 6, 58, 60; schools, 106-108; security measures, 165; self-criticism, 115; social revolution, 33, 154-155; sports, 110-112; standard of living, 11, 26, 92-102, 131, 169, 171; state farms, 100, 111-112; strikes, 18-19, 29, 165; trade unions, 17, 18-19, 42, 111, 163; transportation, 101; treaties broken by, 149-150

spies, Communist, 141-143, 152

Sputniks, 92-93, 114

Stalin, Joseph: Cold War under, 56-67; criminal acts, 44, 47-48, 73, 87, 119-120, 131, 159; death, 65, 67, 69, 76; denounced by Khrushchev, 47-48, 50, 70, 73, 131, 159; denounced by Lenin, 42; dictatorship, 42-44, 47-48; Jewish persecutions, 119-120; plot to kill, 48; purges, 47-48, 73, 87; reaction against, 70-71, 72; religious persecutions, 118; tomb, 72, 73

Stalingrad, destruction of, 52

subversion, 90, 138, 141-143

Suez crisis, 175

summit conference, 77-78

Sun Yat-sen, 124, 138

Supreme Soviet of U.S.S.R., 17, 140

Taiwan, 65, 67, 128, 132, 166, 184

Teheran, peace conference in, 53

Third International, 144-145

Tibet, 6, 132, 179

Tito, Marshal, 65, 70, 84, 87-88, 130, 131, 146

Tomsky, Mikhail, 42, 43

totalitarian government, 13-14, 162

trade, Soviet control of, 149

Trotsky, Leon, 28-29, 32, 34, 36, 42-

43, 48, 49, 85-86, 137

Trotsky, Sedov, 48

Trotskyism, 85-86

Truman, Harry S., 64, 66, 181

Tsar Alexander II, 26, 155

Tsar Alexander III, 27

Tsar Nicholas II, 29

Tsarina Alexandra, 30

tsarism, 26, 29-32, 117, 154-156

Tukhachevsky, Marshal, 48

Turkey, 51, 64, 181

Ukraine, 37-38, 70, 120-121

Ulyanov, Alexander, 27

Ulyanov, Vladimir, see Lenin, Nikolai

United Nations: and Communist China, 131-132; and Hungary, 75; and Korean War, 66-67, 132; and Soviet Union, 60, 66, 76, 82, 161

United States: and Great Britain, 53-54, 81; and Greece, 64, 181; and Japan, 58, 126; and Nationalist China, 126-127, 128; and South Vietnam, 134; and U.S.S.R., 37, 44, 52, 53-54, 57-58, 60-64, 77-82, 131, 150; and Turkey, 64, 181; and Yugoslavia, 65; Communist infiltration, 143; Communist Party, 20, 147-148, 154, 158, 184

U.S. Information Agency, 183

U.S.S.R., see Soviet Union

Voice of America, 184

Warsaw Pact, 75, 146

West Berlin, 7, 60-64, 77-80, 141, 150, 175-176

West Germany, 62, 80, 146

White Russians, 36-38, 48

William, Dr. Maurice, 125

World War I, 25, 30, 33, 34, 144, 156, 179

World War II, 10, 45, 50, 51-52, 56, 76, 107, 116, 126, 127, 138-139, 145, 147, 167, 178, 180

Wrangel, Peter, 38

Wyszynski, Cardinal, 74

Yagoda, Henrich, 48

Yalta agreement, 53-54, 57, 58, 150

youth organizations, Soviet, 109-110

Yugoslavia: and Communist China, 130; and Greece, 64; and U.S., 65; and U.S.S.R., 6, 65, 70, 87-88, 131, 146, 180; collective farms, 19, 87

Zhukov, Georgi, 76

Zinoviev, 42, 48